NEVER TRUST A MAN IN ALLIGATOR LOAFERS

Never Trust a Man in Alligator Loafers

What His Shoes Really Say About His True Love Potential

DONNA SOZIO

CITADEL PRESS
Kensington Publishing Corp.
www.kensingtonbooks.com

CITADEL PRESS BOOKS are published by

Kensington Publishing Corp.
850 Third Avenue
New York, NY 10022

All Kensington titles, imprints, and distributed lines are available at special quantity discounts for bulk purchases for sales promotions, premiums, fund-raising, educational, or institutional use. Special book excerpts or customized printings can also be created to fit specific needs. For details, write or phone the office of the Kensington special sales manager: Kensington Publishing Corp., 850 Third Avenue, New York, NY 10022, attn: Special Sales Department; phone 1-800-221-2647.

Designed by Elsas Design

First printing: October 2007

10 9 8 7 6 5 4 3 2 1

Printed in the United States of America
Library of Congress Control Number: 2007929063

ISBN-13: 978-0-8065-2840-3
ISBN-10: 0-8065-2840-0

This book is dedicated to *Self*ology:
the Art of Loving Yourself.

And to you, my fabulous reader,
whom I love more than you know.

Contents

Acknowledgments

It takes a village to write a book. In my case it also took two continents, three islands, and a 1 percent interest cash advance.

I would personally like to thank my family who loved and supported me from the beginning to the end. Jennifer Parker, my voice of reason. My fabulous network of friends who contributed their Sole Stories. My Starbucks family in Manhattan Beach. Rainbow Sandals and Madison at Fred Segal who embraced the book. My amazing teachers: Jillian Alexander, Dr. Pat Allen, Dr. Bernard Beckwith, Ricki B.B., Charles Carney, Michele Denman, Dorit Dyke, Maria Amparo Escandon, Lee Ettinger, Roger Hamilton, Chris Howard, Har Simran Khalsa, Les Plesko, Tamara Taylor Leigh, Viki King, Adriana Lewis, Amy Perry, Liz and Paul Racy, Edward Sweeney, and Larry Thompson. The UCLA Writers' Extension. TUT.com. Agape. XL Results Foundation. Zappos.com. The Los Angeles Times Festival of Books, which gave me the inspiration to finish my book. My fabulous agent Robert Wilson. My editor Danielle Chiotti who brought me to my highest potential, and copyeditor Bonnie Fredman. Special thanks to my Father, who inspired me with his stories of my favorite fallible superhero. And Mom, I would never forget all my angels stirring the pot for me in heaven. My deepest gratitude. Thank you. Thank you. Thank you.

Note to the Reader

It is my strong suggestion that as you read this book you have some fun and give yourself a good bootie shake. Bring this book to work. Share it with friends. (Definitely shake your bootie with friends.) Pour champagne. Read it in the tub and get the pages wet. Take it camping or to Vegas (great bootie-shaking opportunities in Vegas). Or read it in your favorite shoe store in Paris. Perhaps snuggle up with your honey bunny, discover the Soul of his Sole, and shake your booties together.

And if you find yourself perfectly alone, another fabulous companion to this book is a jumbo bar of imported chocolate. Let it melt a little until it's nice and gooey. It's okay to get chocolate on the pages. I will be disappointed if you don't. In fact, I'm eating chocolate right now.

Donna Sozio

Introduction

May 16, 1989, 15 years old

I was cornered in the freshman quad. My friends were up in arms. Fingers were pointing. "A freshman breaking up with a senior?" They demanded an explanation. I told them the truth: I didn't like his shoes. They all sang out like a Greek chorus: "That's outrageous!" "Ridiculous!" "You can't do that!" "It's petty." "Superficial." "Not nice." "You're supposed to love someone for what's inside. Besides, they're *only* shoes."

In hindsight, I found this an interesting reaction from girls who read their horoscopes daily. But in that moment, I didn't have the foresight to explain that judging a man by his shoes is loving him for what's inside. In fact, it's one of the best ways to discover what's inside a man, and it's easier to interpret than his star chart. But I shrank under their accusing fingers. I was afraid to trust myself. I believed instead what the Doubting Daisies said, "They're *only* shoes," and began mistrusting my own reactions and intuition.

May 16, 2005, 32 years young

There were many things I didn't understand at fifteen—what were boys about, how to do algebra, and why my parents wouldn't buy me a *new* car. And in that moment standing in the freshman quad, I didn't understand the most essential truth of all: when I judge a man by his shoes, I'm tapping into something powerful. Me!

Judging a man by his shoes isn't petty, superficial, or unkind. It's smart. What a man puts on his feet aren't *just shoes.*

They're concrete evidence, the physical manifestation of what lies beneath. Go ahead. Do it. I dare you. Judge a man by his shoes. Do it because it's fun. Do it because it's an adventure in discovering as much about you as it's learning about him. You're the real reason behind relationships anyway. That's right. You! Relationships are all about you and whom you decide to be in a *relationship* with to whoever is lucky enough to date you.

When you find a man with shoes you adore, does that mean he'll stay with you forever? No. Does it guarantee he'll never hurt you? Nope. There are no guarantees when you're dealing with *other people.* But that's not the point. That's the adventure!

In your romantic adventures, you want to have as many tools in your toolbox as possible. Judging a man by his shoes is definitely an ace up your sleeve. It not only answers your relationship questions but also teaches you to trust your intuition. Some women believe the answers to their relationship questions are written in the stars. Perhaps. Yet, there is a simpler solution. Look down. The Soul of his Sole is standing right in front of you.

Definition

Other People—*A constant source of challenge, confusion, and annoyance, yet also the possibility of satisfaction, joy, and enlightenment.*

NEVER TRUST A MAN IN ALLIGATOR LOAFERS

PART ONE

Introduction to Soleology: The Art of Judging a Man by His Shoes

Q: *What do shoes have to do with romantic relationships?*
A: Everything.

Shoes are meant to be in pairs. When shopping for shoes, you ask the salesperson for its mate. Would you ever mismatch your shoes? No! Then why mismatch yourself to a man? Shoes live side by side—sometimes in tight boxy spaces. And just like a man, the wrong fit can hurt and make us cry.

If you're going to live together with a man in a box—no matter how big—it's important that you are compatible with your *sole*mate. Soleology helps determine your Solemate Compatibility Factor before you sign a year lease. Even if you fall head over heels in love, judging a man by his shoes helps you remember that relationships are always ladies' choice. Because once you learn Soleology, it's not only the Prince who gets to see if the shoe fits!

Definition

***Sole*mate Compatibility Factor**—*The chances of living together in a box without experiencing spontaneous relationship combustion.*

Before we continue, there's just one little thing: magicians don't reveal their tricks, nor should you. Men love a mystery. So don't tell men about Soleology! Keep it among us girls. Pinky swear? This is because your man's shoes reveal more about who he is at his *sole* level than he is most comfortable knowing about. At the moment, there is a certain innocence and vulnerability to a man's shoes. Frankly, men haven't evolved to the level of shoe consciousness that women have. Keep Soleology on the down low and don't blow it for the rest of us. Make sure it's not a man looking over your shoulder while you're reading this book. And if it is, don't point at his shoes and start laughing. As hilarious as they may be, don't blow your cover. Keep your *shoe face.*

Definitions

Shoe Face—*A woman's all-knowing yet seemingly oblivious facial expression used for the explicit intent to confuse men.*

Sole Level—*The depth of a man's character that his shoes reveal.*

Three ways to keep your shoe face if caught checking out a man's shoes:

1. Expound suddenly on the intricacy of the asphalt, floor tile, or carpet under his feet.
2. Be ready with an answer if he asks, "What are you looking at?" by casually combining "Just your shoes, darling" with a hair toss and a wink.
3. Use sex whenever necessary. It's a great mind eraser, so he won't remember a thing.

CHAPTER 1

Talk Shoe to Me

Sole Note:

A man may wear his heart on his sleeve, but his shoes will tell you what condition it's in.

Men don't always say much. Luckily for us their shoes do. Actually, *shoe talk* is a language in which many women are already fluent. Although men haven't achieved the pinnacle of *shoe consciousness* that women have, it doesn't mean that their shoes talk any less. They just don't know it. And we're not used to listening. At first it may feel like men's shoes speak in a gobbledegook foreign language sort of way. Think of Soleology as your Gobbledegook-to-English dictionary. Nothing is lost in translation because men's shoes only speak one language: the truth.

Definitions

Shoe Talk—*The secret language of men's shoes that reveals his sole level.*

Shoe Consciousness—*The conscious awareness that a man's shoes are the outer expression of his inner character.*

You see, it's no accident that the words sole and soul sound the same. They're related. One is a window to the other. As women, we already know that each pair of shoes we wear communicates a different aspect of ourselves that we feel is worth the credit card bill or pinched pinky toe to express. Although we might be monogamous with men, we never are with our shoes. Which is why women don't think it's crazy to own fifteen pairs of black shoes. We are simply expressing ourselves fifteen different ways.

Although men don't typically own fifteen pairs of black shoes, the truth is that they express themselves through their shoes just as much as women do. What a man's shoes say about him unlocks the mystery of who he is at his sole level. As much as men want us to think they are simple "just love me and feed me" types, they're really just as complicated as women are. Which is why judging a man by his shoes is so important. His shoes tell you who he is—and who he isn't—on the inside. Ultimately, what a man wants to experience from his shoes gives you insight into what he wants to experience in life, including his relationship with you!

The Sole Truth

Men don't always say what they mean. Good thing their shoes do.

THE SHOES: **White alligator-skin, extended-toe, lace-up loafers.**
He says: "I'll call you."
His shoes say: "At 3 A.M."

THE SHOES: **Blown-out, duck-taped thongs.**
He says: "Want to go back to my place?"
His shoes say: "I mean, my van."

THE SHOES: Cream calfskin, designer slip-on, open-back moccasins.
He says: "I don't want to go too deep in right now."
His shoes say: "I'm already too deep in myself."

THE SHOES: Spray-painted black, mid-calf combat boots.
He says: "I'm raging against the machine."
His shoes say: "I'm a ticking time bomb."

THE SHOES: Tommy two-tone suede saddle shoes.
He says: "Do you want to go to a movie?"
His shoes say: "But Mom wants me home by eleven."

THE SHOES: Slick Italian, black leather sandal slides.
He says: "Let's go to the beach."
His shoes say: "I want to show off my legs in my new short shorts."

THE SHOES: Threadbare checkered canvas slip-on sneakers.
He says: "Wanna get high at the laser show?"
His shoes say: "Do you have five bucks for my ticket?"

Definition
The Sole Truth—*The secret language of men's shoes that frequently contradicts the words that come out of their mouths.*

While shopping for shoes, it's quite normal for them to talk to us. It's usually a pair we can't afford or walk in, but the shoes call to us and lock us in on a tractor beam. They pull us closer until we rub their soft strappy leather against our cheeks, and we have to have them. Then you slide a piece of plastic across the counter and they're yours. Simple. Easy. Right?

It's easy for women to listen to what their shoes say about them. Yet, when the shoe is on the other foot—a man's foot—women have blocked out what a man's shoes say about him. And we say men are bad communicators! While it's true that men don't typically have the same orgasmic experience women do buying shoes—which explains why we prefer to buy multiple pairs—the selection process is still the same. Both men and women buy shoes they are attracted to. Once you understand what attracts a man to his shoes, you begin to understand him.

As you decode the secret language of men's shoes, a whole new world opens up that you never noticed before. It's a world filled with insight and intrigue and with messages that are as clear as 20/20 vision. The more skilled you become in Soleology, the more people will take notice and start asking questions such as how did you know he was—lousy in bed, or a good time Charlie or a financial disaster? The answer is that men's shoes have always told you who men are. Only now you're listening to what they say.

As much as there may be evidence to the contrary, the truth is that men care a lot about our feelings. Otherwise they wouldn't have made it so easy for us to find all the information we need to make good relationship decisions. We only need to know what to look for. Shape. Brand. Style. Fit. It all means something. Slip-on vs. laces. Leather vs. suede. Velcro vs. zip.

It all has a charge. Imagine a day without electricity. Once you listen to what a man's shoes say about him, Soleology becomes just as useful in your romantic relationships.

As you discover the benefits of Soleology, don't be surprised if you're overtaken with such a feeling of liberation that you want to tell everyone about your newfound shoe consciousness. Be a Soleology Sister. Spread the good news. Yet, remember that all people are walking their own path, in their own way, and in their own shoes.

Definition

The Good News—*The liberating belief that all is well because men wear the answers to our relationship questions on their feet.*

Soleology Do's and Don'ts

Here are some helpful tips while spreading the good news.

Do judge a man by his shoes.
Don't make rude gestures to men whose shoes you find offensive.

Do tell your girlfriends about Soleology.
Don't try to save them from their boyfriends' "bad" shoes.

Do use Soleology as a conversation starter at parties.
Don't get drunk and rip on every man's shoes you meet at the bar.

Do expand your shoe consciousness.
Don't try to save the world from their own shoes—one shoe at a time.

Do judge which shoes are right for you.
Don't judge which shoes are right for your friends.

Do support your friends through a breakup.
Don't say, "I never liked his shoes anyway."

Do check out all your man's shoes.
Don't break into his apartment when he's not home. (Wait until he's in the shower. Then have a look.)

The Soleology Phenomenon

There are many benefits to listening to what a man's shoes say about him. In fact, your friends will think that you have suddenly *gone psychic* because you stopped going psycho looking for the answers to your relationship questions. Also Soleology saves you time, money, and calories by instantly weeding out the posers, players, and riffraff. Not only is it less expensive than retail therapy, but it will also keep you looking good in your skinny jeans because less *spontaneous relationship combustion* translates into less consumption of triple chocolate-chunk-breakup ice cream.

Definitions

Gone Psychic—*What people will think happened to you when you stop complaining about men because you started listening to what their shoes said about them.*

Spontaneous Relationship Combustion—*The seemingly sudden and unexpected blowup of a relationship due to what seems like unforeseen forces.*

In the relationship game, if you listen to what a man's shoes say about him, you'll know what cards he's showing, know what's missing from the deck, and be able to call his bluff. Dating disappointments be gone. Say farewell to false starts and au revoir to unwarranted bootie calls. Unless, of course, you want one!

Test your Shoe Talk listening skills. First, try these exercises in the comfort of your own home. When you're ready, take it out into the field.

At Home

What do these shoes say to you?

1. Superslide Astrobright rubber garden crocs.
2. Black patent leather ankle boots with sexy side zip.
3. Retro-funk slim sole sneakers with fashion-fast-flash-cool-line design.
4. Poofy beige lace-up leather comfort walkers.
5. Leopard-print twin-tip creeper sneakers.
6. Classic chestnut leather-flanked, solid-sole, master-crafted wingtips.

7. Stubble-trouble sockless high-contrast white leather (tan ankles) loafers deluxe.
8. Flip-flop-a-don't-stop easy-in easy-out summer-of-love sandals.
9. All-terrain, all-weather, high-sierra, high-performance, Velcro-nylon-hybrid hikers.
10. Slim-jim, winter white backless leather leisure loafer.
11. Thick leather and 1001 buckles Man Sandals.
12. Linen lover, open-toe, slip-on leather Caribbean holiday sandal.
13. Show-me-the-money, black-on-white, flip-tip, red-carpet velvet-rope, midnight-express wingtips.
14. King me-Henry-the-8th imperial-fop feathers and velvet "casual" evening slippers.
15. Rubber prickle-sole slip-on burnt burgundy and lime loafers.
16. Real-deal roughrider scuff-me-up leather no-laces work boots.

In the Field

Now, it's time to go outside and mingle with the locals. Go it alone or hold court with your girlfriends in a public place where there's lots of foot traffic. Perhaps, set up camp at a coffee shop, a mall, bookstore, or bar. Then for the next hour or so, look only at men's shoes and listen to what they say about their owners. Take a mental note. Or jot it down.

If you like what you hear, feel free to approach the owner to see if you like what he has to say as well. Odds are you'll be pleased with your results.

CHAPTER 2

Sole Impressions

Sole Quote:

"Well-worn shoes have their wearer's character embedded in them." —Lisa Greenstein, shoe portrait painter

Have you ever:

- Slapped your hand to your forehead lamenting, "I should have seen the signs" after a relationship spontaneously combusted?
- Been upset because you felt like there weren't any signs when a relationship spontaneously combusted?
- Asked for a sign when you thought your relationship was about to combust spontaneously?
- Asked for a second sign because you didn't like what the first sign told you?

If you answered yes to any of these questions, then you're like the 99 percent of all women who didn't recognize, trust, or ignored your sole impression.

Definition

Sole Impression—*That instantaneous feeling you pick up after checking out a man's shoes. Typical reactions are smiling comfortably, gritting teeth, or suddenly scanning for the nearest emergency exit.*

Sole impressions are the feelings you are left with after you check out a man's shoes. These "feelings" are the biggest relationship sign there is. They can hit you like a ton of bricks or be as subtle as raising an eyebrow. Either way, your sole impression will give you all the information you need to decide if you want to move in closer to your date or move to another state. That is, of course, if you trust it.

It's imperative that you learn to trust your sole impression because it's one of the most accurate signs of your romantic future with a man that there is. Most often women overlook their sole impression because they aren't used to men's shoes as signs of what to expect in a romantic relationship. Instead, women expect signs to come in a certain package—like a ring box. We may think other signs are too big, are too small, or come too late to be anything real or significant. Or we wait for a sign to drop out of the sky instead of walking in the front door. Yet, if you just look down—you'll find two of the most accurate relationship signs standing right in front of you.

The good news is that you don't have to physically put your ear next to a man's shoes to listen to what they say. You only have to be open to the signs a man's shoes give you to "catch" your sole impression. Most often women discard their sole impression before they even realize that they caught it. It's like there's an automatic "reject" button that goes off inside our heads when we catch the first sign of unpleasant news from a man's shoes. Sometimes, we want to be in a relationship so badly that we're not going to let a "little thing" like his shoes stand in our way. But listening to men's shoes is never a roadblock to romance. Instead, your sole impression is more like a trusted tour guide offering you "been there done that" insight into the romantic possibilities with any particular man.

At first becoming aware of your sole impression may feel

like trying to catch a slight "blip" on a radar screen. And when something about his shoes makes you go hmm—the information being offered may feel a little uncomfortable. Even itchy. Because when you're not ready to listen to your sole impression, you let excuses kick in to make you feel better about his shoes. Perhaps he just lost his job. Or his grandma died. Your mind starts looking for whatever excuse to help you get over his vegan hemp wraparound walkers, green-eyed snakeskin boots, winter white leather huaraches, or Weejun wonders.

It's exactly this point, while trying to convince yourself why you shouldn't care about his shoes, when you know that you have caught your sole impression! This usually happens when you pick on something you don't like about his shoes. Because when your sole impression is all green lights, you're usually too busy looking into his eyes to notice that you're feeling hot and heavy over not only him but also his shoes.

Just like first impressions, sole impressions come full circle. This is because they communicate aspects of a man that he won't ever tell you. Men's shoes offer you a sneak preview into your future. They're like a "man manual" because the shoes a man chooses to wear are a mini-him. Just as water in a jar has the same properties of the river, a man and his shoes are in essence the same. When you look at his shoes, you're really seeing aspects of him reflected in his silver sneakers, mojo moccasins, alligator loafers, or fluffy bedroom slippers. You haven't met the man wearing the shoes I just described, but you already *caught a feeling* just from their description. That's your sole impression. And your sole impression will tell you if his alligator loafers are friendly—or if they bite.

Once you begin catching your sole impression, trust it.

Feel confident taking action from the signs you receive. Feelings don't just pop out of the air. They come from somewhere. You feel a certain way about men's shoes because just like a little transistor radio, they give off a signal and you pick it up. If his shoes make you want to run for the hills—don't walk—run for the hills! When it comes to romantic relationships, there are many things we don't know. We don't know if the man we fall in love with will stay with us forever. We don't know if he will suddenly become obsessed with noir movies, steal our eyeliner, or worse—our shoes! But the one thing women *do* know about relationships is how they feel about them—every moment of every day. And when we meet a man, whether we admit it or not, we know exactly how we feel about his shoes.

Sole Story

Dana loves to take walks. Especially down memory lane. As much as she reminisces about past boyfriends, she reminisces about their shoes. This is when Dana came to the not so surprising conclusion that all the men whom she loved the most also wore the shoes that she loved the most.

Her favorite tale to tell is about her college boyfriend Sam. His uniform was a great tan jacket with elbow patches, a clean white fitted T-shirt, brown leather belt, and the perfect pair of matching brown leather loafers. In the three years they dated, Dana claims that he owned at least five pairs of these shoes. Sam knew what he liked and kept going back to what worked.

Sam wore his favorite shoes with confidence and style. That's exactly how Dana remembers feeling next to him—confident and stylish. He let his shoes wear in just enough to give off a subtle sense of ruggedness. But the moment they were run down, he bought another pair. Sam used the same approach in their relationship. The space between them was comfortable, yet he never let it get old. His shoes were just as consistent and approachable as he was.

Signs, Signs, Everywhere Signs

It's nice to know what to expect from other people because it gives us a sense of comfort and security. Especially when it comes to romantic relationships. In fact, this burning desire is so universal that calling Madame Zora at $1.95/minute has become an international multibillion-dollar industry. Men's shoes are also an international multibillion-dollar industry. We just haven't tapped into it—yet.

It isn't a far stretch to compare Soleology to other "accepted" organized systems of fortune telling. Take astrology for an example. Astrologists assign personal qualities and aspects to a star date. Soleology assigns personal qualities and aspects to a man's shoes. Each star sign lives in a house. Soleology considers the shoes men wear like their own little houses for their feet.

Chances are you're already using a man's star sign to help guide you in your romantic relationships. When you ask a man "What's your sign?" what you're really asking is, "What can I expect from you?" Are you a sex god Scorpio? A stubborn Taurus? An indecisive Libra? Emotional Pices? Or an All About Me Leo?

Instead of paying for a thirty-minute reading of his star sign, when you judge a man by his shoes, you get your sole impression for free *within* the first thirty seconds that you meet him. Your sole impression answers the very same question, "What can I expect from you?" This is because everything we do, say, or think leaves a record or an imprint in the world around us. When you look at a man's shoes, you're seeing the sum total of everything he has said and done for him to arrive in those particular shoes, in that particular place, at that particular time. Whether or not you believe the answers to your relationship questions are written in the stars, he's wearing two of them on his feet. It doesn't matter if you're a firm believer in signs, why not dabble a little just for fun? I bet you read your horoscope this month—just for fun.

If you're wondering what type of home you'll be living in with your man, just glance at his shoes. The type of home he provides for his feet is directly related to the type of home he will provide for you.

Home for His Feet	***Home for You***
Off-roading rugged-terrain hikers	A pup tent for two, complete with rain flaps and an air mattress. Now that's luxury.

Baja-style flip-flops	Prepare for a pimped-out palapa.
No-slip-grip beige leather deck shoes	The ultimate in waterbeds—you've got a liquid backyard as far as the eye can see.
Tie-me-down, missionary-style, lace-up leather oxfords	Nothing wrong with a white picket fence.
Zebra-print disco dancers	Home is on the dance floor or on your couch.
So-supple designer cream backless leather slip-ons	A so-supple designer cream-on-cream penthouse luxury suite.
Cowboy boots	An expansive ranch in Wyoming or a cramped Hollywood apartment. It depends on whether he's made it as an actor.

DR. SOLE

Q. *I was brought up to judge men by the inside, not the outside, of their shoes. That just sounds weird. What should I do?*

A. Innately you know that what you see on the outside is a good idea of what you get on the inside. That's why you choose one apple over another—and take two hours getting ready. Yet, if you feel that looking deeply into a man's shoes is a little kooky, consider the other places we look for signs of our romantic future: Wet tea leaves. Coffee grounds. Tarot cards. Your love line. Picking off flower petals. □

Don't worry, you're not alone. It's not just the romantics who look for signs to guide them. Sailors read clouds to predict the weather. Surfers read the surface of the water. Rock climbers read the mountain. Lawyers read a jury. Analysts read polls. So why not read men's shoes? Remember, that just about everything we try for the first time feels a little weird until we get used to it. Then it becomes as much a part of our life as water or chocolate. Try to imagine life before cell phones, e-mail, or nonfat chai tea lattes. At first, we might have resisted. We didn't want to become one of *those people.* Now it's hard to remember life without them.

Definition

Those People—*People who annoy you at first by doing something new until you try it and discover that you can't live without it either.*

The Way to Catch Your Sole Impression

At first your sole impression is like the shy quiet girl in the corner of the classroom who seldom raises her hand but has all the answers. She's the perfect person to make friends with when a big test is coming up in the romance department. Your sole impression may feel very subtle in the beginning because all the information you pick up from a man's shoes boils down to a feeling. In order to harness the power of your sole impression, you must train yourself to become aware of these feelings. Put your sole impression alert on high because important romantic information is downloaded in an instant. Which also speeds up the Poser Weed-Out Process. Since your time is valuable, Soleology helps you save a whole bunch of it by weeding out the posers from the get-go.

Definition

Poser Weed-Out Process—*A woman's mental elimination of men who don't live up to their shoes.*

When a man tries to pick up on you, it's not only his attitude but also his attitude toward his *shoes* that you pick up on. When it comes to shoes, men are into their feelings just as much as women. They choose what shoes they wear because they want to feel a certain way. That's what you pick up on. Intuitively you know if his shoes are all talk or if they walk the walk. It's your sole impression that tells you if he's a vegetarian cowboy or if his shit kickers are fresh off the ranch.

Once you start catching your sole impression, you'll learn more about men than you ever knew was possible! Men's shoes are on men's feet everywhere and come at us from all directions. It's like treating yourself to a sign buffet. There they are, right in front of you, just hoping you'll pick them up. If your sole impression catches a whiff of something that doesn't smell right, inquire further. Which doesn't mean that you actually need to smell a man's shoes. Just by looking at them, you can usually smell a rat. Once you start weeding out the posers, psychos, energy suckers, and tightwads with just the flicker of your eye, your friends will think that you have gone psychic.

But in reality, you have just become a better listener—to your self.

Whenever you try something new, inevitably there will be a learning curve. If you ever experience any difficulty honing in on your sole impression, try these troubleshooting techniques:

Problem: Hazy Sole Impression.
Solution: Compare your date's shoes to a car.

1. You already know what kind of a car you'd jump into. Perhaps it's a Cadillac, Hummer, Minivan, or Mini Cooper. Or it could be a Camero, Jaguar, Monte Carlo, or Gremlin.
2. Next, look at your date's shoes and ask yourself, "Would I take a ride in them?"
3. Then stand back as your sole impression comes flying through the neon lights and smoke-machine haze.

Problem: Mixed Signals
Solution: Learn to think like a shoe.

1. Before you let another man's shoes walk into your life ask yourself, "If I were a shoe, what kind of shoe would I date?"
2. Describe its style, purpose, shape, color, and feel.
3. Next, describe what shoes you absolutely wouldn't date. What is their style, purpose, shape, color, and feel? What shoe qualities repel you? Why?

4. Then ask yourself, "How would I feel if a shoe I would never date tried to make out with me?"
5. Note your physical reaction. Cringing is a no-go. Yet, if you can image yourself making out with his shoes, you could be a pair made in heaven.

The next time you are at a meet and greet, remember the perspective thinking like a shoe gave you. Expect every man you meet to live up to your *shoe expectations.* Because what you won't put up with in a shoe, you shouldn't put up with in a man.

Definition

Shoe Expectations—*The boundaries you set that define what you will and will not put up with in a man's shoes.*

First-Response Reactions

While catching your sole impression, it's important to notice not only your thoughts but also how your body reacts to his shoes. *First-Response Reactions* to a man's shoes offer just as much information as the shoes themselves by telling you how you feel about them instinctively. If you suddenly find yourself making the sign of the cross with your fingers as you back away from his shoes, it's pretty clear how you feel about them, which means it's a good time to reconsider how you also feel about *him.*

Don't feel you have to know why your shoulders shot to your ears when you discovered a pair of faux leopard loafers or ankle half boots. And don't feel bad that you did. For the moment, let it be enough to know that you reacted to that situation and there was good reason for it. You just might not know why—yet.

Definition

First-Response Reactions—*How your body intuitively reacts when you come in contact with a man and his shoes.*

Typical First-Response Reactions

You like his shoes:

- Your arms uncross and relax comfortably by your sides.
- Your breath slows to a pleasant rhythm.
- You inch in closer.
- You twirl your hair and cross your legs toward him.
- You lick your fork seductively.
- You think about what shoes you'll wear to your wedding.
- You wonder what your kids will look like.

You don't like his shoes:

- You suddenly feel nauseated.
- Your body turns into a pretzel.
- Your breathing becomes short and rapid.
- Your eyes scan for the nearest exit.
- Your mind attempts Truth Judo.
- You imitate *The Scream.*
- Your shoulders suddenly attach themselves to your ears.

DR. SOLE

Q. *I went with my sole impression and finally found a man who I adore just as much as his shoes. Why then does he still manage to piss me off?*

A. First of all, congratulations with going with your sole impression. You won't regret it. Second, keep in mind that trusting your sole impression doesn't guarantee men will always behave the way you want them to. Men still have a little something called free will. No matter how much we want to take it away—we can't. Anticipating your romantic future with a man doesn't mean that you control him. Instead, trusting your sole impression opens you up to a range of possibilities that you can expect from your future solemate. Besides, if your relationships were already perfect—there would be nothing left to do. Just like when a guy is a doormat, perfect can get boring pretty quickly. ☐

As you begin to catch your sole impression, you can expect to meet a little resistance. Like a third wheel, there's someone who'll pop up and try to wedge herself in between you and the solemate of your dreams. That's your *Doubting Daisy.* Your Doubting Daisy is the voice inside your head who says, "Judge a man by his shoes? They're *only* shoes! Come on! Don't be so superficial. Where's that nice girl your mother brought up?"

Actually, it's quite easy to identify your Doubting Daisy because she is very predictable. She loves to use words like "only" or "just." For instance, they're *only* a pair of shoes. It's *just* a body in the trunk. It's *only* a bad feeling. Or it's *just* a small criminal record. Sound familiar?

Before you think you're going crazy "hearing voices," let me be the first to tell you—we all hear voices. There's a

Doubting Daisy inside all of us. And when we introduce something new into our lives—like Soleology—she can set off the smoke alarm in our head. Doubting Daisies are afraid of change—especially when it comes to the *Great Unknown of Relationships.* Rather than opting for the adventure of a new romantic relationship, your Doubting Daisy would rather you stay at home on a Saturday night and watch *Friends* reruns. Or she'll try to convince you to stay in a romantic situation that's "comfortable" even if it doesn't make you happy. Your Doubting Daisy will do everything in her power (exactly why you shouldn't give her any) to make you doubt your sole impressions. It's not that she doesn't care. She does. Only her knees start knocking when she thinks you're heading into uncharted relationship territory.

Definitions

Doubting Daisy—*Any voice living inside your head or beyond that tries to keep you from your heart's desire because it is afraid of change.*

The Great Unknown of Relationships—*The risk of the unknown, yet unlimited possibility for happiness, when you decide to let* other people *into your life.*

Technically, your Doubting Daisy isn't a problem unless you believe the excuses she cooks up for you not to trust the signs a man's shoes give you. If while trying to catch your sole impression she's making a ruckus, try these Doubting Daisy relaxation techniques. First soothe her. Gentle hushing noises will reassure your Doubting Daisy that everything will be okay. If that doesn't work, attempt the bait and switch. Give her something else to occupy herself with like a chocolate cupcake while you focus on the important information your man's shoes are telling you. Another way to keep your Doubting Daisy out of your hair is to send her on a luxurious tropical vacation far, far away.

If you're still having trouble, start a Doubting Daisy cooperation calendar. Draw in happy faces for all the days she cooperates and sad faces for all the days she tries to sell you a lemon. When she does cooperate, think of a fun reward for the both of you. Perhaps get a mani/pedi. Or take a trip to your favorite shoe store, treat yourself to a few new pairs, and then take them home for a delicious multiple shoe experience.

The good news is that while trying to catch your sole impression, there is someone you can always count on. That's your intuition. She will always tell you the truth about men's shoes. Your intuition isn't afraid of change. She's ready for every adventure and listens to the signs men's shoes give her. Your intuition knows your heart's desire and is ready to help you find it. The more power you give your intuition, the more power she has.

You see, Soleology isn't just the Art of Judging a Man by his Shoes. It's also The Art of Trusting Your Intuition. When you start believing that your intuition is as real as any universal fact you read in a book, it is. Just like the earth is round, the sky is blue, and muscle weighs more than fat—the power of your intuition is real. Besides, the more you trust your intuition, the less you will get run over by *the relationship mack truck*.

Definition

The Relationship Mack Truck—*What it feels like you have been leveled with after spontaneous relationship combustion.*

Since love is blind, your sole impression helps you see. Consider it your flashlight in the dark. It illuminates and reveals aspects of a man you previously didn't see yourself. Although Soleology isn't a crystal ball, it's the closest thing to it. Imagine being able to see men from your blind spot. Your insurance rates won't go down. But if you open your eyes to the signs men's shoes give you, you won't be left in the dark.

While trying to catch your sole impression, look who's talking!

Your Intuition	***Your Doubting Daisy***
Yes! I can do it!	I don't know. I've never done this before.
Of course, they'll love me!	I hope they like me.
Of course, I'll get the guy!	Gosh! There sure are a lot of women here.
I look great!	Everyone here is so pretty.
Is it just me or is everybody smiling?	Why is everybody smiling?

MOD: Your Intuition vs. Your Doubting Daisy

Your intuition is the ultimate super sleuth. It wants to know the answers to important questions like why is there a hole in his sole? And get to the bottom of it quickly. While your Doubting Daisy is willing to settle for some quick and cheap attention. When catching your sole impression, you want to be clear who you're listening to. Here are a few examples to help you see the difference.

Your Intuition: Wait a minute! Are his shoes hobo, hippie, or hipster?
Your Doubting Daisy:Who cares? At least he's talking to me.

Your Intuition: Can I fly with his metallic leather lift-off silver sneakers?
Your Doubting Daisy: Hey, at least he wants to take me somewhere.

Your Intuition: Wow! He's as friendly as his Aloha Hawaiian-print canvas slip-ons.
Your Doubting Daisy: He probably lives in Hawaii, and he won't want a long-distance relationship.

Your Intuition: Oh la la. What fabulously expensive shoes!
Your Doubting Daisy: Oh dear, his shoes look *expensive.*

The Zen of Soleology

Soleology says: There is balance in all things. Men have upper-body strength. Women have their intuition. Once you start trusting your intuition, don't be surprised if a feeling of Zen-like calm comes over you. You might feel like a feather floating over a pond, enjoying the ride, yet not worrying about whether you get wet. To experience the Zen of Soleology, you must strengthen your intuition. Your intuition is like any muscle. You must use it to build strength.

When you think about it, men don't doubt their strength. They don't say that it's *just a muscle* or wish it would stop getting so big and strong. Instead, men buy gym memberships, drink protein shakes, and bench-press hundreds of pounds to work their muscles to the max. Besides, how sexy is a man with muscles? Now, imagine how sexy you'll look flexing your intuition. Men love it. Trust me.

Definition

The Zen of Soleology—*The peace that passes understanding when your sole impression tells you everything you need to know about a man to make good relationship decisions.*

A Conversation with Yourself: Your Own Little Radio Show

As women, we're used to our shoes talking to us. Now you're learning to listen to what a man's shoes say as well. If you're a little nervous about having your first conversation with your intuition about a man's shoes, here are a few cool ways to break the ice:

1. Use general introductions like "Intuition, what do you think of his white leather side-zip ankle boots?"
2. Pick a man's shoes that you aren't interested in and hold court inside your head to discover the reason why.
3. Do the opposite. Pick a man's shoes that attract you and pinpoint why.
4. Discuss with your intuition the evolving trends in men's shoes. For example, Is pleather the new leather?
5. Take you, yourself, and your intuition to a men's shoe store and dish up on what you'd like to see on a man's feet and why.
6. Finally, don't forget that the reason we talk is to be heard. Make sure to listen to yourself as well.

If at first your intuition seems a bit sluggish, a bar of imported chocolate is always a good incentive to get it moving again. Your intuition can't get fat, and you'll be working off the calories anyway doing your intuition exercises.

Throughout the day, use your intuition to answer simple questions like:

- Where are my keys?
- What's that noise?
- Who's on the phone?
- Why is he wearing those shoes?

Intuition Muscle Test

How turned on is your intuition? (choose one)

En Feugo!
Steaming!
Hot
Warm
Tepid
Faint
Limp

CHAPTER 3

The Sole Truth

Sole Note:

People tell you who they are.
You only have to listen to what they say.

It isn't just your Doubting Daisy who can be a major roadblock to meeting the solemate of your dreams. Old beliefs can be just as much a barrier to arriving at your desired romantic destination as a dead end. Usually when something unpleasant happens to us once, we say *never again. Never again* will I date a man in prickly-pear French tickler soles with an adjustable Velcro strap. *Never again* will I fall for a man in laceless "distressed" canvas, rubber-toe slip-ons or lounge-lizard side-zip half boots. Perhaps these distasteful events with the men who wore those shoes happened one, two, maybe twenty years ago? Yet, we're still holding onto our *never again* attitude. Which actually means we're still thinking about his shoes even if in a negative way. Which doesn't help us to find the solemate of our dreams, because the opposite of lost love isn't hate. It's moving on.

Think about it this way: Imagine not cleaning behind your fridge for ten, twenty, or thirty years. Uh huh. Yuck. Dirt builds up. Fear, doubt, and judgments do too. The good news is that here is a way to wash it all away and make everything clean, new, and shiny again, which means it's time for Soleology's Deep Thought-Clog Cleanse. This cleanse isn't a liquid diet. Nor will it make you spend a week on the toilet.

Instead, it's more like taking a walk down memory lane. As you walk, you pick up pieces of yourself you left behind and leave behind pieces that weren't yours to pick up. The Deep Thought-Clog Cleanse brings you back to the time before our thoughts got clogged with fear, self-doubt, and painful experiences with men and their shoes.

Once we clean out the *thought clogs* caked on our mind, we can get back to that *free-flowing thinking feeling* we experienced being barefoot in the park as kids—because minds really are like drains. They flow better when open. So, roll up your sleeves. Put on your heavy-duty gloves. Get ready to get down and dirty as we Debunk the Junk. Remember, there are no free lunches. Scrubbing Bubbles and Drano do not work on emotional Thought Clogs.

Definitions

Thought Clogs—*Old icky globs of fear, doubt, and judgment caked on our minds.*

Free-Flowing Thinking Feeling—*The freedom you experience in life when you trust yourself.*

The Way to Debunk the Junk: The Deep Thought-Clog Cleanse

While roto-rootering your Thought Clogs it's good to know what kind of an animal you're dealing with. Soleology documents four of the most common Thought Clogs that can keep you from trusting your sole impression to its full capacity. That is, of course, only if you let them.

THOUGHT CLOG #1: IT'S NOT "NICE" TO JUDGE A MAN BY HIS SHOES.

This Thought Clog typically was handed down to us from grade-school teachers or nuns who taught us that it wasn't nice to judge a book by its cover. Well, they forgot to mention that although it may not be "nice" to judge what book is right for someone else—when it comes to your own life, it isn't wrong to judge who or what is right for you. Especially when it comes to which men you allow to walk into your life. You don't need a black robe or a law degree to give yourself the authority to decide who or what is right for you. But don't believe me. Judge for yourself.

Walk On: Practice Judging for Yourself

Imagine that you have your own televised afternoon courtroom drama. There you are under the bright lights—looking just gorgeous, I might add—listening to each man make his case and judging (gavel and all) whether you will let him into your world. After making their case, if you do let them in, they must be wearing fabulous shoes that indicate good things to come. But if their shoes don't cut it—the door is closed. Bam! No one else knows the secret knock and cannot get in.

THOUGHT CLOG #2: THEY'RE ONLY *SHOES.*

This sounds suspiciously like something your Doubting Daisy would say. Also, it's a popular phrase among those who are afraid to make decisions for themselves based on what their sole impression tells them. Then if you don't like where you landed in your romantic relationships, your Doubting Daisy will come in and try to convince you that you're a *victim.*

The good news is that you're not a victim. You can stand on your own two feet and make decisions based on what feels right for you—including how you feel about a man's shoes. Feelings don't just pop up out of nowhere. Neither does rain mysteriously drop from the sky. They both come from somewhere. So does your sole impression. You feel a certain way about a man's shoes because you picked up a vibe that they gave off. Remember, even though we can't see electricity (or our feelings), we know when we've been shocked.

Definition

Victim—*Anyone who has temporarily forgotten that she is more powerful than anything she is afraid of.*

THOUGHT CLOG #3: WHAT YOU DON'T KNOW ABOUT A MAN'S SHOES CAN'T HURT YOU.

When confronted with something that trips your "everything's cool" cord, some women take a *truth trip* to outer space. Perhaps they think that if they don't know what's going on in their lives, they're not vulnerable to it. Yet, it's better to walk in the light rather than be in the dark. That way you won't get tangled in his tassels, run over by angry Dr. Martens, or bit by a disagreeable pair of croc mocs.

When it comes to finding the solemate of your dreams, screw hindsight. Who cares if it's 20/20? No more do you have to go through a breakup to have a breakthrough. Instead, develop your foresight. Investors make fortunes anticipating future markets. Why not hit the relationship jackpot?

Definition

Truth Trip—*Where we go when we mentally check out of life when we don't want to face the truth about men's shoes.*

THOUGHT CLOG #4: MEN ARE BAD COMMUNICATORS.

The truth is that men are excellent communicators, but they're not always good with their words. Which is why we need to judge them by their shoes. That way, we can learn the lesson before we get *gum face*.

Definition

Gum Face—*What happens when you keep blowing hot air into a situation you know is getting sticky and eventually will pop.*

Thought Clogs Be Gone

Saying good-bye is harder for some than it is for others. Especially if your Thought Clogs have been with you a long time. Some of us are ready to fling them off like yesterday's news. Yet, for those of us who feel we want a more ceremonial approach, Soleology offers a few suggestions:

1. Write all your Thought Clogs down on a piece of paper and burn them. Or rip them up and flush them down the toilet. Watching them turn to ash or swirl down the drain can be very satisfying.
2. Stand on top of a mountain and shout, "I am Thought-Clog Free" as you beat your chest Tarzan-style.
3. Take a shower and sing from the top of your heart, "I washed those Thought Clogs right out of my hair."

4. Rearrange the furniture in your house to remember that you have a new attitude.
5. Play "New Attitude" by Patti LaBelle on repeat at full blast until the police come. Then have drinks and appetizers ready so that you can invite them in and check out their shoes.

When getting rid of Thought Clogs, rinse and repeat as often as you feel necessary. And for those particularly nasty ones, combine Patti LaBelle's *New Attitude* with Jennifer Beal's *What a Feeling!* Flashdance Tuck! Run! Burst! and Leap! dance. The shower dance sequence is optional.

OOPS-A-DAISY

Are there any other Thought Clogs you want to get rid of? If so, write them here. Then rinse and repeat any of the steps, and shake them off for good.

____

____

____

____

The Culprit: If Not You . . . Who?

Since we're all telling the truth here, let's go a little deeper. It's not always a Thought Clog keeping you from the truth about what a man's shoes say about him. It could be you!

Avoiding the truth is like playing with one of those elastic paddleballs you win at the county fair. No matter how hard you hit the ball, it keeps bouncing back until it knocks you over the head and you're all tied up. Which is all the more reason why you should trust your sole impression—so we don't look ridiculous trying to duck the truth in our romantic relationships.

Soleology documents several ways we commonly do it. Duck the truth that is. Each of these is not recommended and guaranteed not to work. Ducking the truth will only keep you from experiencing the romantic relationship of your dreams. Just like ducking under the limbo stick, you can only go so low before you fall splat on the floor. Although we may try to avoid the truth, men's shoes don't. If they can handle it, so can we.

SOLE TRUTH DUCKING TACTIC #1: HOCUS POCUS

As much as men can be masters of illusion, sometimes we play hocus pocus on ourselves. Women have a tendency to take what a man says and put it into the context of what we want his words to mean. For example, when a man says "I love you," we immediately translate those three little words into what we want them to mean. Perhaps you're suddenly married with two gorgeous children who never cry and you still have the amazing body of a twenty-one-year-old. Yet, just because he says "I love you" doesn't mean it's exactly on par with how you want him to mean it.

Women have a tendency to do the same thing with men's shoes. It's an important distinction to make because the "fantasy jumps" we make in our mind vs. the reality check of the situation isn't always exactly on par with how you imagine it to go. So when you check out a man's shoes, keep your feet on the ground. Because when you fantasy jump, it isn't your sole impression. It's more like a knee-jerk reaction when you think you can get something you want for free.

Fantasy Jump vs. Reality Check

The Shoes	***The Fantasy Jump***	***The Reality Check***
Rock Star boots	Backstage passes	Garage band with high school buddies
Tuxedo shoes	Ready for marriage	Works at a mortuary
Earth sandals	Professional protester for Green Peace	Hard-line Republican
Summer slides	Time-share in Bermuda	Time-share gigolo for golf widows

Bling Bling loafers	Ring bling	Dot Bomb . . . his shoes are all that's left
Deck shoes	Sail me around the world	Sails a dingy
Pro Basketball sneakers	Hoopside seats	Drives a hooptie

If a man says, "I love you," and you love his shoes, try not to do the translating of the meaning yourself. Logically, you know the words form a sentence. It has a noun, a verb, and a direct object of attraction. But it isn't a complete thought. Instead, it's more like a dangling participle. Make men finish their "I love you" thought. After he says it, make the "and" gesture. Then wait for him to make the "what?" gesture. This may go back and forth a few times until you finally get an answer.

Once you have that answer, make yourself finish your "I love his shoes" thought. Do you love his shoes because they represent worthwhile loving qualities in a man? Or do his shoes represent material things you think you're going to get from him out of the relationship? It's important to be clear with both translations from the get go because you don't want to be crooning solo to the lyrics of "Love Don't Live Here Anymore."

Alternative meanings for the infamous phrase, "I love you."

I love you *right now.*
I love you *because I'm lonely.*
I love you *like pizza.*
I love you *like spaghetti.*
I love you*r enormous breasts.*
I love you *because my girlfriend just left me.*

SOLE TRUTH DUCKING TACTIC #2: NOBODY'S HOME

When the truth is out there, some women like to slip into their Truth Protection Suit, which looks like a cross between an orange HAZMAT coverall and an astronaut outfit. Its sole purpose is to incubate you from any unpleasant feelings, such as what a man's shoes are telling you when you don't want to hear what they say. While a Truth Protection Suit temporarily provides refuge from whatever it is you don't want to face, it is about as liberating as being locked in a closet.

When your man is wearing a pair of shoes that you just can't stomach like a pointy ankle boot or a city slim sneaker, instead of donning your Truth Protection Suit, take Pat Benatar's approach. Let his shoes hit you with their best shot. Because the truth is that you are more powerful than anything you are afraid of.

SOLE TRUTH DUCKING TACTIC #3: TRUTH KARATE

There are all types of martial arts: karate, aikido, and kung fu. Yet, one of the most commonly used—although not officially recognized—form of martial arts is Truth Karate. This is when women karate chop away from themselves anything they don't want to see or hear such as the truth. Expertly done in one-down-chop fluid motion, most Truth Karate Masters don't ever realize when they've karate chopped the truth away from themselves, except when it starts boomeranging back from all directions. That's why it's best to lay down your truth-chopping karate arms. That way when it comes back around, it won't hit you in the head.

SOLE TRUTH DUCKING TACTIC #4: ESCAPE AND EVADE

Have you ever made yourself so busy that there just wasn't time for the truth? Yet, the only schedule truth keeps is your own. Wherever you go, there it is—sitting on the couch, in your bank account, in your e-mail. In fact, truth is the ultimate stalker, and to date, there are no laws against it. Like the tax man, it just keeps coming back until you are all settled up. The best way to avoid a truth audit—which is never pretty—is to set a weekly appointment in your daily planner and make yourself available to the truth about your man's shoes in your romantic relationships.

SOLE TRUTH DUCKING TACTIC #5: HOLY LINT!

It's remarkable how lint on your sweater can suddenly take on incredible importance when faced with a truth that you don't want to hear. A miniscule bit of fluff becomes the focus of your world rather than the information a man's shoes are trying to relay to you. The incessant picking at it is usually accompanied by a glazed-over facial expression. It's interesting to observe that as soon as the shoes trying to relay the truth get frustrated and walk away, the glazed look disappears. Instantly, all interest in said piece of lint is lost. While attempting to face the truth about men's shoes in your romantic relationships, make sure all your garments are already lint free.

The Truth Is Good for You

When you let the truth in about a man's shoes, you may realize a liberating sense of power you have never experienced before. This is similar to the metamorphosis women experience on the dance floor at weddings when the DJ plays Gloria Gaynor's "I Will Survive." During these *moments of truth* do not be rattled. Do not put on your Truth Protection Suit or high kick the truth far, far away. Remember, your Doubting Daisy has a mute button. Press it.

Instead, slip into your sole impression like a nice warm bath. Sit quietly. Breathe. Let it sink in. Feel it. You are more powerful than anything you are afraid of. Let your intuition guide you to what you desire in your heart. You intuition will tell you if you are caught in a shoe fantasy or if your Prince Charming is the real deal.

Soleology Truth-Avoidance Rx:

Don't wait until a wedding to listen your power song.

1. Write down what truth you are afraid to face about his shoes on a piece of paper.
2. Play "I Will Survive" over and over until you know you will.
3. Play "I Will Survive" over and over until your hot new neighbor pounds on your door.
4. Check out your neighbor's shoes.
5. Know that either way it's a win/win.

CHAPTER 4

Your Sole Perspective

Sole Note:

Both shoe shopping and man shopping can be equally satisfying.

Once you start trusting your sole impression, shopping for men in the relationship department of life can be just as much fun and enjoyable as shopping for shoes. Just for a moment, think about why women love buying new shoes. You walk into your favorite shoe store and there they are—hundreds of shoes all on display for your pleasure. In fact, the entire shoe department was created just for you and this moment together. The shoes on display are hoping you pick them up and try them on for size. You narrow down your selections and give some a whirl. How do they feel? Fabulous? Like a glass slipper? Or do some pinch? Even just a little? And when you find a pair—or two—that makes your heart sing, you walk out of the store swinging your shopping bag with an *after-shoe-shopping-glow*, certain that you're about to begin a wonderful relationship with your newfound shoes.

Yet, what about men? You have a favorite place to shop for shoes. Where is your favorite place to shop for men? Perhaps it's downtown just after the five o'clock bell as men are loosening their ties looking for a nice quiet place to relax? Is it the beach so that you don't have to wait to see them with their shirts off? Perhaps at a fund-raiser where you can suss out what shoes he wears when he's feeling generous. Just like your favorite shoe store, pick a place where there is a high percentage so that you'll find at least one, two, or three men that you'll like.

Wherever you land in the Men Department of Life, shopping for a man can be the same wonderful experience as shopping for shoes. It only depends on your *sole perspective.* Consider each man you meet as you would a new pair of shoes. There they are—standing in front of you—just waiting for you to pick them up and try them on for size. Just like you try on a pair of shoes before you buy them, your sole impression lets you "try on" the man to see how he might feel in a relationship together. Can you imagine yourself standing next to his shoes for the rest of your days? Can you imagine yourself standing *in them* because in relationships what's his becomes yours. Or do they pinch a little, and you're hoping that they'll stretch or change?

Definitions

Sole Perspective—*The point of view a woman develops when she realizes that shopping for a man can be just as fabulous an experience as shopping for shoes.*

After-Shoe-Shopping Glow—*The utter feeling of satisfaction as you walk out of a shoe store knowing that a whole new experience awaits you in your new shoes.*

DR. SOLE

Q. *Help! My sole impression and first impression are conflicted. What do I do?*

A. Do not worry. This is totally normal and bound to happen. You may be attracted to a man's shoes but not the man. Or you are attracted to the man but not his shoes. This is because the information a man's shoes tell you may be different from what he is telling you. While only you can decide which voice to listen to, remember that men's shoes only speak one language: the truth. Men, however, can be much fancier with their words. Generally speaking, how you feel about a man's shoes now is how you will feel about him in the future. This is because the shoes he chooses to wear on his feet represent the sum of all the choices he has made in his life thus far and most likely will repeat. If you are still in doubt, then just ask him, "Why are you wearing those shoes?" Your time is valuable. The sooner you get your answers, the sooner you get what you want in a man *and his shoes!* ☐

Sole Story

On paper it seemed that Connie's first date with Paul was going quite well. He picked her up when he said he would. He took her to dinner and a movie. He even asked Connie out for a second date. Everything looked good. That is, until Connie filled in the details.

Standing in line for dinner at Panda Express, Paul busted out two expired coupons and hassled the cashier until she accepted them. Over two-for-one chow mein, Connie considered overlooking Paul's "If It's Free It's for Me" attitude because she was really attracted to his shoes. They were fabulous. A rich nutty brown mock toe casual wingtip and stylishly cut. Yet their date continued on the fast track downhill. Paul refused to pay for parking so that Connie walked three blocks in her four-inch stiletto "limo shoes" to the theater. Once at the theater, Paul's teenage neighbor gave them VIP treatment. He let them in for free and walked them to the front of the popcorn line.

Connie was baffled. How could Paul be so cheap and have such amazing taste in shoes? Connie decided she needed to dig for some more information. She casually mentioned to Paul that she liked his shoes. "Cool," he said, "my client gave them to me after her husband died. You know her husband and I had something in common." Paul winked. "We're both a size thirteen." They weren't watching a horror film, but the fact that her date was walking in dead man's shoes was scary enough to make Connie bolt for the door.

Truth and Consequences

WHAT HAPPENS WHEN WE DON'T TRUST OUR SOLE IMPRESSIONS?

How many times in a relationship have you waited for proof of what you already "just knew" months, sometimes years, before you decided to do something about it? This is what happens when we don't trust our sole impressions. We feel that we need to look outside ourselves to validate what we already knew from his shoes in the beginning. When women don't listen to their sole impressions, the consequence is that they are left without recourse to answer their relationship questions other than to employ some less-than-respectable fact-finding methods—like snooping, stalking, breaking into his e-mail—or worse. Women not only deserve answers to their romantic relationships but they're entitled to them. The question is, By what methods?

Since the beginning of time, women have pawed through men's things looking for signs of what to expect—or not to expect—in their romantic relationships. Although it is commonly referred to as snooping, the "technical" name for it is Awareness Expansion. Soleology offers an Awareness Expansion alternative to snooping with none of the side effects and better results. When you trust your sole impressions, you will never need to become—albeit borderline—criminal in a relationship again.

Definition

Awareness Expansion—*Extending your knowledge past what you think you already know about a man through any variety of legalesque methods.*

Now, you can answer all your relationship questions while respecting yourself and the law. It's time we put to rest our snooping and stalking behavior. No more sticky fingers. No more sneaking around. No more getting caught. Now, we can walk in the light. Men conveniently wear shoes in the open air so "technically" Soleology can't be considered snooping. And rather than pawing through his drawers, when you trust your sole impressions, you can put your black catsuit to better use.

Another consequence of not trusting your sole impression is that we can become really annoying. Innately, women know that being informed is a good thing. That's why we ask men a thousand questions: *How was your day? What did you do at work? Who was on the phone? Why haven't you called? Why are you looking at me like that? Who's number is this? Where were you last night? Working late again? Where were you last night? Are you upset? What's wrong? What do you think of us? How come you don't answer your cell? Why are you wearing cologne to work? What was that look for? Who was at the party? Why do you smell like a brewery? Did you know what today is? What do you mean you're not hungry? Is something wrong?* We ask so many questions when they can all be answered with a single one: Why are you wearing those shoes?

If you find yourself traveling or dating an international import, no problem. Bring this book with you so you can ask, "Why are you wearing those shoes?" in nine different languages. Don't worry if you can't understand their answer. Your sole impression is a great translator.

Spanish: ¿Por qué usted está usando esos zapatos?
French: Pourquoi portez-vous ces chaussures?
German: Warum tragen Sie jene Schuhe?
Italian: Perchè state portando quelle scarpe?
Dutch: Waarom draagt u die schoenen?
Portugese: Por que você está desgastando aquelas sapatas?
Russian: почему вы носите те ботинки
Swedish: Varför er du slitande den här skön?
Greek: Γιατί φοράτε εκείνα τα παπούτσια;

High Speed vs. Dial Up

It's time to upgrade your awareness expansion methods from dial up to a high-speed hook-up. There is new technology available to answer all of your relationship questions without getting sticky fingers.

Soleology vs.	**Snooping**
Fresh data	Old diary
Relationship legal	Relationship misdemeanor
All the information you need	Caught red-handed, empty-handed
No naked pictures of ex-girlfriends	Naked pictures of ex-girlfriends
Trust building	Builds mistrust
Makes interesting conversation	You can't bring it up
No explanations needed	Call your lawyer
Nothing to confess	Plead innocent

DR. SOLE

Q. *Help! I'm a snoop-a-holic. I can't stop. What do I do? I don't trust my boyfriend.*

A. Although you don't feel like you trust your boyfriend—the real question is do you trust yourself? It's our mistrust of our own feelings that sends us looking outside ourselves and into his drawers to find our answers. We read men's diaries and *drive by* just to see if they're home when they said they would be. We might even call back odd numbers in his cell phone. Yet, all this snooping is just to look for concrete confirmation of what we already know from our sole impression. Because if we didn't already know something was fishy, our fingers wouldn't be inside his coat pockets. Before you snoop, ask yourself: Do I already have the answers I'm looking for? Usually the answer is yes. ☐

When we hit a wall always looking for outside *proof* of what we already know in our romantic relationships—ultimately we ask for help. Help comes in the form of a Relationship Vital Sign. The first Relationship Vital Sign is of course your sole impression. Yet if you're not ready to listen to what men's shoes are trying to tell you about their owners, life will get the information to you some other way.

Sole Impressions vs. Relationship Vital Signs

Sole Impressions	Relationship Vital Signs
Things are going well.	
I like his shoes	He brings me flowers.
I like his shoes	He calls between 10 A.M. and 10 P.M.
I like his shoes	He met the parents.
I like his shoes	He proposed.
I like his shoes	He still brings me flowers.
Things are not going well.	
I don't like his shoes	He calls between 10 P.M. and 10 A.M.
I don't like his shoes	He never brings me flowers.
I don't like his shoes	He hasn't called.
I hate his shoes	He disappeared.
I hate his shoes	He took my checks and disappeared.

Definition

Relationship Vital Signs—*The various ways life tries to give us a "heads-up" in romantic relationships when we ignore our sole impression.*

Rather than waiting for Relationship Vital Signs to hit you over the head, trusting your sole impression is a kinder, gentler way to get your relationship answers. If you don't like his shoes, as time goes by, most likely you won't like other aspects about him as well. Perhaps you won't like his jokes, or how much he drinks, or how he didn't tip the waiter. Before the situation escalates, you should listen to your sole impression. That way you get less drama and much more action.

Rush Hour in the Men Department of Life

Trying to navigate the hundreds of men's shoes in a fast-paced elbow-to-elbow social setting, like a bar, can feel like driving down the freeway at rush hour—in Rome. In this case, use your sole impression just as you would a street sign. When you get a *green light feeling*, move forward. Or if you see a red flag waving over his feet telling you there's sticky traffic ahead, hit turbo boost or peel out.

Definition

Green Light Feeling—*A feeling of knowingness that the direction you're heading in a relationship is getting you closer to your heart's desire.*

Paying attention to street signs certainly reduces everyone's chances of a crash. It also increases your chances of a safe arrival to your destination of choice. Yet, what if no one followed street signs? Especially during rush hour. What would your driving experience feel like? Confusing? Dangerous? Nerve wracking? Perhaps that's what your dating experience feels like? Confusing. Dangerous. Nerve wracking. But dating doesn't have to feel like this. Your sole impression gives you directions in the form of insight into how to get to where you want to go quickly and with whom you want to travel, which is good because backtracking sucks.

Soleology's Relationship Backtrack Principle

You're at Relationship Point *A*
You want to be at Relationship Point *B*
Your rate is *x*

Distance Traveled / Rate = Time Invested

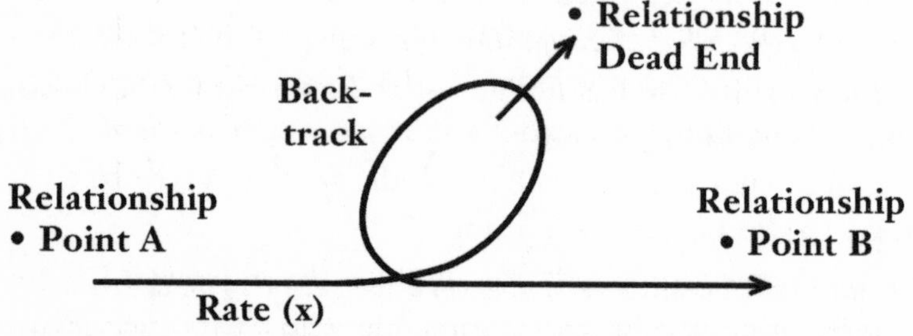

As you cruise along the Relationship Highway of Life, watch for the signs his shoes give you.

Green Light feeling = hit the petal to the metal. You are on course.

Yet, if his shoes are a red flag . . . if they tell you Relationship Point B is actually the other way and you keep traveling in the same direction, prepare for a dead end.
In the case of a Dead End, double Time Invested. Change the value to Time Lost. And factor out Experience Gained.

Now decide:
Was the Experience Gained > Time Lost?
Or < Time Lost?
You do the math.

The Soleology Truth Card

While letting your sole impression drive in the singles scene rush hour, every woman should know a couple of quick maneuvering tactics to avoid dating some really bad shoes. If your sole impression picks up a red flag and he's not responding to your polite indications that your sign is *closed*, then you've no choice other than to pull the Soleology Truth Card. It works like a charm every time.

Tell him, "I'm sorry but your shoes are hideous. I simply can't imagine myself dating someone who wears such awful shoes." He'll be stunned. He won't know what to do or where to put the information you just dealt. He'll pause in disbelief. Take advantage of this moment to get away.

The Soleology Truth Card is such a flip on the "it's not

you, it's me" cliché that he'll never see it coming. Although be warned that it'll leave an imbalance. If he's daft enough to wear such hideous shoes, he might try to equalize the situation by turning it into an "it's her not me" thing. Prepare for him to come back with some lame insult about how you "look fat in those pants" (which you don't). Don't let his flimsy retort rattle you. Simply shrug your shoulders and move on. Remember, the point of the Soleology Truth Card is to get his shoes out of your space as soon as possible. That way you free yourself up for the man who just walked in wearing a pair of shoes you can't wait to meet.

Definition

Red Flag—*An imminent feeling of doom upon evaluating a man's shoes.*

Sole Story

Mary met Chris at an underground club. Within the first few minutes, she managed to get him to stand under one of the few lights to check out his shoes. They were lovely. Amazing leather. A solid sole and super sleek. But there was a glitch. A hitch that itched. They were long and skinny. The tips flipped. They were too lovely. His shoes said feminine. Yet, Mary liked everything else about him, so she entertained the thought of dating her first metrosexual man. They locked lips and she gave him her number.

On his first date with Mary, Chris wore a sharp shirt and hip jeans. He pulled the outfit together with another fabulous pair of shoes. The leather was shiny and textured. A good start, but again they were long and skinny with little thin laces. They almost came to a point at the toe. Mary heard them say the same thing: feminine. This time the hitch itched a little more. But she put her sole impression aside and proceeded with the date. Chris opened the door for Mary, and she slid inside his pearly white car with creamy beige leather seats. The car struck her as eerily familiar—until Mary remembered that her grandma owned the same ride.

Over dinner, Chris was very attentive. He didn't let the check burn a hole in the table before he picked it up. Yet, as they left the restaurant, Mary caught him checking out his butt in the entrance mirror. She gave him a quizzical look. He gave her a quizzical look back. "What?" he said, "I just got these jeans."

Mary ignored his shoes for three more dates. It wasn't until Chris called from a business trip in Miami and asked her for the name of the hair gel she used that Mary finally listened to what his shoes had been telling her for weeks. He was too metro for her to consider him sexual.

DR. SOLE

Q. *Soleology sounds too good to be true. Aren't relationships supposed to be hard?*

A. Once you start reading the signs a man's shoes give you, it may feel like you're cheating in your romantic relationships. It may feel like Soleology is too easy. Perhaps you were taught, "Anything worth having doesn't come easy." Throw that old adage out the window. That kind of thinking was so 1990s. This is the twenty-first century. Listening to what a man's shoes say about him isn't cheating. It's a *shortcut*. You no longer have to take *the long way* in relationships. Being open to the signs men's shoes give you about a man's romantic potential gets you where you want to go in your relationships quickly. If you still won't let yourself off the "it's too easy" hook, think about this. No one complained that the first washing machine was too easy. Go on—feel good about a shortcut. You deserve it! □

Definitions

The Shortcut—*A luxury ride down the relationship express lane through careful analysis of a man's shoes.*

The Long Way—*The unnecessary uphill climb when we confuse romantic relationships with hardship.*

PART TWO

Soleology: How It Works

Do you remember Reagan's Trickle-Down Theory in the 1980s? Well, it may not have worked with economics, but when it comes to men, the *Relationship Trickle-Down Theory* is spot on. Whether we realize it or not, we are all being *trickled on* by our significant other. A man's relationship with himself trickles down onto every other relationship he has. That includes his relationship with his shoes (yes, men have relationships with their shoes) and his relationship with you. When it comes to being trickled on in a relationship, you definitely want more than the weekend forecast.

All women have questions in their romantic relationships. Should I stay? Should I go? Why does he do *that thing* that bugs me? And when do I get to use the remote? The good news is that men's shoes are here to answer them up front instead of down the road. Yet, there are four Pre-Relationship Questions you should ask before even entering one:

1. Who is he, really?
2. How does he feel about himself?
3. What can you expect from him in the relationship?
4. What can you expect from him in bed?

Chapters 5–8 show you how your man's shoes can answer each of your Pre-Relationship Questions. This is because how a man treats himself is how he treats his shoes. And how he treats his shoes gives you an accurate forecast of how he will treat you. So if you're tired of being trickled on, keep reading. Soleology offers the best insurance policy you can't buy.

Soleology's Relationship Trickle-Down Theory

Man's relationship to Self
Man's relationship to his Shoes
Man's relationship to You

Definitions

The Relationship Trickle-Down Theory—*The inevitable effect your man's relationship with himself and his shoes has on his relationship with you.*

That Thing—*Repetitive acts of continuing annoyance that men commit without relent like leaving the butter out, the toilet seat up, and underwear on the floor.*

Trickled On—*The inevitable fate of dating as you make yourself vulnerable to* other people.

CHAPTER 5
Archetypes

Sole Note:

Cops, strippers, and doormen shouldn't be the only ones who benefit from the careful analysis of men's shoes.

When we tell our girlfriends about any great guy we just met, we usually run down his *man stats:* his name, job, car, hair, and height. Whether he rents or owns his home, and how close it is to the beach or downtown. All these answers are meant to explain who he is to our friends. Yet, the problem with these answers is that they tell us what we already know in the first five minutes of conversation or just by looking at him. It's a good start, but it's not enough to decide whether to give a man our valuable time and attention.

Definition

Man Stats—*How a man gets reduced to a series of numbers and statistics that are supposed to answer the question who is he so that your friends can give you the thumbs-up or the thumbs-down.*

However, listening to what a man's shoes say about him tells another story. His shoes will give you the answers to the questions that you really want to know. This way it won't take you a year or more to find out if his idea of a romantic evening is you, the boobtube, and a cheap brewski. While running down the typical man stats to your girlfriends helps, you know who he is superficially, only his shoes can tell you the truth about who he is, *really*.

The first step is to determine his *arch*etype. In the old days when there were fewer choices in men's shoes, men were limited to more functional footwear like the Dutch clog, Wellington work boot, Egyptian reed sandal, or corporate wingtip. But times have changed and they keep on changing. Conventional roles and boundaries are being bent and broken by the minute. Today there are almost as many archetypes as there are men's shoes on the market.

Whatever your man's archetype, it tells you what type of life experience he's living out through his shoes. Which shoes your man decides to wear every morning answers the question, "Who do I want to be today?" Let's see, relaxed and casual or rich and flashy or adventurous and spontaneous or rigid and uncompromising? Then he chooses his shoes accordingly to fulfill his desired feeling. Whoever said men weren't into their feelings certainly wasn't talking about men's shoes.

Definition

Arch**etype**—*Classifications of shoes that reveal a man's deep unconscious patterns of behavior that are expressed and relived through his desire to own and be seen in said particular style of shoe.*

Soleology divides a man's archetype into four different archetypical categories: Work, Play, Sport, and Fantasy. While considering how your man's shoes fit into each category, remember to factor in not only the shoe itself but also his attitude toward it. Is he true blue, letting the situation define his shoes? Or does he color outside the lines and his shoes define the situation? The latter would be the kind of guy who wears flip-flops to the beach *and* the office. While our true blue only feels like he can fly at work in wingtips.

Once you discover which categories your future loverman's shoes fall into, you are well on your way to answering the first Pre-Relationship Question: Who is he *really*. If the answer fits like Cinderella's slipper, you just may have found the solemate of your dreams. And get ready to ride off into a sunset of an everlasting *after-relationship glow.*

Definition

After-Relationship Glow—*The wonderful feeling of satisfaction when you played your cards right, anted up, and won your heart's desire.*

Sample Archetypes

If life is a stage then we are all playing a part. The good news is that in life we get to pick who we want to play. When you pick apart a man's shoes, you are really learning about his character. Perhaps even more than he knows himself.

Work

Oxford Numbers Guy
Tickle My Tassel
Wingtip Wonder
Croc Moc Alpha Shoe

Play

Open-Toe Free-Flowing Spirit
Old Skool Rules Skateys
Euro Sandal Summer Slide
1001 Buckles That Jingle Jangle Jingle

Sport

Amphibious Adventure-Man Land/Water Crawlers
White-Bread Wonder Power Walkers
Rapper's Delight Every-Man-Can-Jump Sneakers
Urban-Jungle City Hikers

Fantasy

Exotic-Print Ankle Bootie Man
White Loafer Disco King
Sockless and Sexy Miami Heat
Captain Stubing Canvas Slip-On Deck Shoes

Archetype Category: Work
Represents: Authority

A man's work archetype represents how compliant he is with authority. The concept of authority is key in romantic relationships because when a relationship becomes a power struggle that's exactly what it is—a struggle—which can certainly chip away at any after-relationship glow and make being trickled on feel like acid rain.

Every place of work, whether it's a construction site or a downtown law office, has a dress code for the sake of professionalism or safety. How compliant or rebellious your man is with his shoes toward the dress code at work is a sign of how he deals with authority. Soleology divides the aspect of work into three archetypical categories: Yes, Sir!, Limit Pushers, and Rebels.

AUTHORITY ARCHETYPE #1: YES, SIR!

When your man's shoes comply with the dress code at work, generally it's a good sign that he respects authority. He puts his personal agenda aside and works toward the greater good. He may not like the shoes he wears on the job, but he goes along with it for safety reasons or for a professional look at the office. Yet, compliance can be tricky. If your man is compliant with a job he doesn't find satisfying, it can turn into resentment. Ask yourself how much of his compliance means compromise? Does your man find genuine satisfaction in his job? Or is he suppressing his artistic tendencies in middle management?

It's important to know what percentage of his compliance translates into resentment because just like plaque, resentment builds up. And it doesn't take long for things to turn ugly. If your man is satisfied with his career shoes, being in a relationship with him may feel like being in Barbarella's pleasure machine. Yet, if he's a bubbling volcano of molten resentment, your relationship could feel more like being trapped in a threesome with Hurricane Katrina.

One way to discover his resentment level is to consider his

attitude toward the shoes he wears to work. Does he resent his shoes? Does he call them his "Monkey Shoes?" Or is he happy to put them on? Also, what happens in those moments just before he puts them on? Is he grouchy and spiteful or playful and relaxed? Notice the moments just after he gets off work. Does he keep flip-flops in the car to change into? Does he kick off his work shoes at the door? Or does he prefer to maintain his professional look at happy hour or at home? Let no sole go unturned because all your *sole sleuthing* adds up to complete the *man puzzle* and answer all your relationship questions.

It's important to note that being a Yes, Sir! archetype doesn't automatically translate into being a kiss-ass or an eager beaver toward authority at work. That depends more on your man's perspective of what his job stands for. Some men really believe in their company. For instance, your Yes, Sir! Man could wear traditional Mexican rope sandals and be an environmentalist working for the natives in San Juan Ignacio that lands him behind bars.

Definitions

Sole Sleuthing—*The unique ability of women and their inquiring minds to catch a sole impression of men's shoes.*

Man Puzzle—*The Aha! Moment women experience when they put all of his pieces together and see the big picture.*

Where do your man's shoes land on Soleology's Authority-Resentment Meter?

Burning Inferno!
En Fuego!
Hot!
On high!
Medium
Low Simmer
Tepid
Cool

AUTHORITY ARCHETYPE #2: LIMIT PUSHER

If life is like a box of chocolate*s*, so are limit pushers. You never know what you're going to get. Except, of course, if you read the little insert that tells you exactly what you'll find inside each chocolate. Which is just what Soleology does with men's shoes and it will come in handy when you find yourself in love with a limit pusher. Limit pushers are men who are still experimenting with boundaries. Whether it's good or bad, they wear shoes looking for a reaction. They haven't found themselves in the Yes, Sir! world, yet they aren't ready to commit to being a rebel either. They're standing with one shoe on either side of the authority fence.

Typically, you can spot a limit pusher when you look down, raise an eyebrow, and ask yourself, "He's going to wear *those* shoes?" While his shoes don't totally offend, they do ruffle a few feathers. His shoes walk the line, so you're left wavering back and forth wondering whether you should say something.

Your man may wear black sneakers to the office or hiking boots to a job interview. Either way, if you're dating a limit pusher, keep the Trickle-Down Theory fresh in your mind. If a man is testing the water with authority at work, most likely he'll test the water with authority in his relationship with you. When this happens, you may want to remind your limit pusher of the Relationship Golden Rule. When you're happy, he's happy. Ultimately, this makes women the authority in relationships. That is, of course, if you know how to work it.

If you're dating a limit pusher, the relationship will test your backbone. Like a rocket ready for takeoff, limit pushers are in a prime position to experience tremendous growth and change. Or they can be just getting their rocks off. If it's hard to tell, conduct a litmus test. Exert your authority over something quasi-insignificant, like dinner. Insist on Italian if he wants Chinese. If he's pushing the limit just for kicks, the acid level will rise and you'll know whether you need to get takeout—for one.

AUTHORITY ARCHETYPE #3: REBEL

There's no denying that rebels are sexy. They deliberately break the rules without fear. Rebels know who they are and what they want, and they won't settle for less. It's unfathomable for anyone to tell them what they should do or who they should be. If a rebel's boss doesn't like his shoes, he doesn't care. He knows someone else will.

It isn't necessary to have spiked hair or wear combat boots to be a rebel. Rebels come in all sorts of shapes, sizes, and varying degrees of *rebel relativity.* For instance, if your man's father is a Boston Blueblood, he might refuse to wear loafers. Or if his parents are vegan hippies and own a hemp farm, to be a rebel, your man might make a point of wearing calfskin loafers to Christmas dinner. It isn't just the shoe itself but the intention behind wearing them that makes or breaks a man's rebel relativity.

Definition

Rebel Relativity—*The degree to how a man uses his choice in footwear to make a statement about what he can't stand or stands for.*

If you find yourself dating a rebel, make sure that both of you feel rebellious about the same issues. Perhaps you both got fired for wearing Dr. Martens to your office day job. Or he takes the David Beckham approach and doesn't care if what was traditionally *hers* now becomes his. All is fair in love and war when you and your man express a mutual rebellion. Yet, the waters divide when he doesn't care about the same things that you do. And if you find your man suddenly rebellious toward *you*, expect some troubles to trickle down into your rebel paradise.

In such a case, a relationship with a rebel can become a one-way lonely street. As much as it's sexy to be fearless and uncompromising, you may have to remind a rebel that he still lives on a planet inhabited with *other people.* Women fall into that *other people* category, especially if you're dating him. A rebel's "my way or the highway" attitude is cool if he's the only one left in the Twilight Zone. To maintain a functioning relationship with a rebel, you may need to become somewhat of a rebel yourself. Put your foot down and remind him that a relationship consists of two people, or he can do his rebel yell alone.

Yet before you make any sudden decisions, perhaps there is a way your man can feed his rebel tendencies and keep his job. Traditional *bad boy* and *mountain man* shoe companies have recently come out with a softer gentler line of shoes that your rebel can get away with wearing at work. Then he can keep the edgy rebel image of the brand without the questionable hooks, spikes, studs, or animal print. Because when everybody is happy, everybody wins. Rebels included.

Sole Story

Sheila has owned her company for fifteen years and has much experience hiring and firing. When it comes to hiring, she always judges men—or anyone else—by their shoes. She explains that it's her way of telling if a person is congruent. If an applicant tells her one thing but their shoes say another, she knows she needs to dig deeper to see if they're telling the truth.

While interviewing a man for a high-level sales position who wouldn't only generate new clients but look after existing clients as well, Sheila noticed that his shoes weren't well cared for. The leather was dry and cracked. His soles were worn down on the sides. And the plastic at the ends of his laces were split and frayed. Although he looked good on paper, Sheila followed her intuition and kept looking for a candidate who could first look after his or her shoes and her clients.

Years later at a business dinner with some female

colleagues, they were discussing some of the best and worst employees they've had over the years. After the third glass of wine, Sheila wasn't surprised to learn that her colleagues had similar stories about employees and their shoes. They all noticed one similarity: all their worst employees had the worst shoes!

HOW TO SPOT A YES, SIR! OR LIMIT PUSHER OR REBEL MAN

Put your sole impression to the test. The chart below will help you determine a man's archetype at work.

	ARCHETYPES		
	Yes, Sir!	Limit Pusher	Rebel
The Shoes	*Attitudes toward them*		
Flip-Flops	Hey, I own this company.	It's casual Friday.	I'm getting fired on Friday.
Clogs	I'm an iron chef.	These are Mogs . . . the man clog.	I don't care if I look gay. I am!
Tevas	I'm a river guide.	I fell in a river once.	I *am* the river.
Tasseled Loafers	I'm going for a raise.	I'm raising the bar.	My parents are hippies. I'll get a raise and a rise.

	Yes, Sir!	Limit Pusher	Rebel
The Shoes	*Attitudes toward them*		
Penny Loafers	Collars up!	No collars.	No shirt.
Wingtips	I love my power suit and shoulder pads.	Don't laugh. The tips are better.	Okay, but they're all I'm wearing.
Spray-Painted Dr. Martens	I'm a creative.	I'm in middle management, okay? But I'm still a creative.	I don't care where I work. Don't tell me what to do. I'm an f–ing creative.
Backless Slip-on Oxfords	If my boss wears them, so do I.	Ha! My heel is naked.	Business in the front. A party in the back.
Black Leather Sneakers	I'm an engineer. We all wear them.	They're black. No one will notice they're sneakers.	So bad they're good. Well, almost. But I'm a rebel. I don't care anyway.
Vans	So stoked to work in the surf industry.	They're loafer-like.	I've worn these since the summer of '69, and I'm not stopping now.

Where do your man's shoes land on the Soleology Authority Continuum?

The Soleology Authority Continuum: Work

Archetype Category: Play
Represents: Vulnerability

A man's playtime shoes reveal his *armadillo aspect*, which not only shows how comfortable he is with his vulnerability but also demonstrates his openness to himself and the world around him. Some men are able to let go and be free. Others like to retain elements of structure and authority, even in their playtime shoes. When it comes to men expressing their vulnerability, Soleology offers three archetypes: Open and Free, Comfortable yet Secure, and A Modified Loafer.

Definition
Armadillo Aspect—*The amount of underbelly a man allows himself to express through his shoes.*

VULNERABILITY: ARCHETYPE #1: OPEN AND FREE

Spontaneous and fun, an Open and Free Man wears shoes that feel like the next best thing to bare feet. If his feet can't be naked in the sand, he at least likes to feel his toes wiggle in the breeze. You won't find a buckle, tassel, or shoelace in sight. His shoes are uncomplicated, and he can kick them off in an instant. No lengthy unbuckling process is necessary. Plus, the worn-in leather feels like a second skin.

Open and Free men are generally easygoing and are as inviting as a golden retriever. They enjoy a natural flow and are happiest when they aren't confined or strapped down. When your man is wearing his open and free shoes, the only thing he wants to command is going commando.

Types of Open and Free Man Shoes

All flip flops
Open-toe Birkenstocks
Athletic Sport slides
Over the top leather slides
Open-toe hybrid hiker

Yet his open and free-flowing feeling could mean he likes his relationships easy breezy too. If you're holding on too tight and he feels his spirit is constrained, don't be surprised if he slinks away in the middle of the night and takes his shoes with him. Or he disappears on an extended surf trip to Baja. One way to prevent his imminent escape is to give his open-and-free attitude its due respect. And give his footwear some respect while you're at it. It's not hard to do when you accept that his open-and-free shoes have most likely been around longer than you have. By understanding an Open and Free Man's shoes, you show that you understand him.

If you find yourself attracted to an Open and Free Man, know that despite his easy breezy attitude toward life, he might become quite attached to his footwear. A good pair of flip-flops requires some pain up front before they earn his respect and, after time, mold to his feet. Then he and his shoes are one. They co-exist together in perfect harmony for years. Perhaps that's why when his favorite flip-flops break down, so does he, as one would because they were as familiar and comfortable as a childhood friend.

Which is why Open and Free men usually keep their old favorites alive with duct tape well past the point of resuscitation. Letting a beloved pair of open-and-free shoes go can be as painful for them as putting a favorite pet to sleep. When this happens, you can also expect a mild "transitional" depression, as he mourns his last pair while breaking in the new ones. And just like a new puppy, a new pair of open-and-free shoes may never quite fill the void of the old faithfuls that passed away.

While dating an Open and Free man, the object of the day isn't to make him settle down. Instead, consider him wild and exotic game that doesn't fare well in captivity. Although settling down might happen by default, you never actually want to use those words with an Open and Free archetypical man. Instead of snagging or snaring him, you want to create an "environment" of freedom and adventure in your relationship. This type of man needs to feel space and freedom in his relationships rather than boundaries and limits. This may at first seem like it would work against you. But it doesn't. A man wears his open-and-free shoes when he wants to feel the same way. If that describes how he spends the majority of his time, then he has to feel that way in the relationship if you want him to spend the majority of his time with you. Only then do you *have* him.

Another thing you have going for you is that when you play your open-and-free cards right, the loyalty that these men feel toward their shoes will also trickle down onto you and your relationship. Perhaps put the shoe on the other foot—yours—and discover an open-and-free experience together. Buy yourself a corresponding pair of his favorite shoes, and he just might love you forever.

Sole Story

Jennifer's husband always told her that he loved her more than anything. She found this to be true until the day Tom left his Rainbow Sandals on the beach. It was more than an hour on the freeway before Tom realized they weren't on his feet or in the beach bag or in the car. This was Jennifer's first experience with a man losing his foot's best friend. Much to Jennifer's surprise, Tom had a complete meltdown.

"Don't worry," she said, "we'll get you another pair." Tom's face twitched and he shook his head. "Turn the car around," he said. "We're going back. I need my Rainbows."

Tom was silent the whole way down. He looked like a wounded child who had just lost his favorite blanky. When they arrived back at the beach, Tom jumped out of the car without a word. Triumphantly, he returned a new man with his Rainbows in hand. Tom was smiling and breathing again. He gave Jennifer a big hug. "Thanks, honey," he said, "I knew you'd understand." When they returned home, Jennifer was relieved too. If there was going to be another woman in her relationship with Tom, at least it was pair of shoes.

If your Open and Free Man's shoes come to an unexpected end, there might be some fallout. Here's how to avoid a blowout emergency:

- Keep a spare pair of his favorites in your tote bag.
- Circulate new pairs in for birthdays, holidays, and anniversaries.
- Sign up for their local drop ship program.

If none of these work, give your Open and Free Man a bag to breathe in and call the twenty-four-hour Emergency Blowout Hotline. 1–800–Blow–Out.

VULNERABILITY ARCHETYPE #2: COMFORTABLE YET SECURE

Okay, so he's not a total bohemian, nudist, or Burning Man veteran. But he definitely likes to be comfortable when he's not at work. His shoes are made from soft natural fabrics. Supportive and functional, they certainly let in some air and light. Worn with or without socks, you will find a wide array of buckles, snaps, or Velcro to tuck in his feet for a snug fit.

The quintessential Comfortable yet Secure shoe is affectionately known as the Man Sandal. Just like Seinfeld's "Manziere" opened up a whole new world of possibilities for men in terms of comfort and support, the Man Sandal opened doors for the Comfortable yet Secure Man by exponentially increasing his footwear choices. A throwback to the Greco-Roman days, the Man Sandal offers men a whole new frontier in summertime footwear. And just as the Romans did, these shoes swing both ways. The Man Sandal covers the gambit from overly masculine to overly feminine. Whichever way your Comfortable yet Secure Man swings in his Man Sandals is a sign as to where he might be overcompensating—somewhere, somehow.

The Comfortable yet Secure Man isn't the type who'll sell all his earthly belongings on a whim and take off to Costa Rica. But don't count him out on an adventure either. Only he may prefer to shop for his adventures online or via a four-color print catalogue.

Relationship-wise, a Comfortable yet Secure Man can be quite conflicted. Underneath it all, he yearns to be more like his Open and Free friends but buckles himself down in his shoes. Although, in some cases, it's the security of the shoe that gives him the freedom to fly. Like a kite on a string, he enjoys the flight but also likes to be reeled in.

VULNERABILITY ARCHETYPE #3: A MODIFIED LOAFER

A Modified Loafer Man defines himself through his work whether he's in the office, in Bermuda, or in the bathroom. There may not be much of a transition between his work and playtime shoes except for a tassel or two. Dressy casual wins on even the laziest days and a perennial PDA attached to his hip keeps him locked in the business loop. To cool things down a bit, he may change out of his cream linen pants for a pair of cream linen Bermuda shorts. But no matter what the outfit, the shoes remain the same. Consider yourself lucky if he takes off his black dress socks.

Most Modified Loafer men combine business with play. In

fact, most consider business play. Whether it is competitive golf, conquer-and-kill sports such as game fishing, exotic hunting, or corporate takeovers, like a game of chess, they are testing the mettle of their colleagues just as they would a competitor, which is why their shoes are usually very, very expensive. They certainly don't want to be *out-shoed* by the competition.

Definition

Out-shoed—*A feeling of shame and defeat when another man receives more status from his shoes than your man did.*

When considering a relationship with a Modified Loafer Man ask yourself if his idea of play is how you enjoy spending your playtime too. If the answer is no, that doesn't necessarily mean that you shouldn't be together, only that the relationship may work better if you play separately. It could also be that your Modified Loafer Man has been working for so long that he has forgotten how to play. Since all work and no play makes any man dull, why not slip a surprise pair of open-and-free playtime shoes into his closet. Call them his "remember when" shoes and see what happens. Your Modified Loafer Man may suddenly take some time off and take you to Hawaii, or he may decide to cash out, buy a yacht, and cruise with you the rest of his days. You never know.

HOW TO SPOT AN OPEN AND FREE OR COMFORTABLE YET SECURE OR A MODIFIED LOAFER MAN

Put your sole impression to the test. Match the shoe and the attitude expressed by it toward his armadillo aspect to determine a man's archetype at play.

	ARCHETYPES		
	Open and Free	Comfortable yet Secure	A Modified Loafer
The shoes	*Attitudes toward them*		
Garden Shoes	I'm walking on cement, but I can still smell the roses.	The best part about them is the back strap.	My stylist said they make my legs look good.
Flip-Flops	Nothing feels better.	No back strap?	Never let anyone see you sweat or see your feet.
Relaxed Loafers	I definitely have the Monday flu.	It's Sunday. I'd better set my alarm.	I love the smell of Monday in the morning.
Sneakers	Where are my toes? I can't feel my toes.	Comfortable and secure. Nice.	Does Gucci make a sneaker?

	Open and Free	Comfortable yet Secure	A Modified Loafer
The shoes	*Attitudes toward them*		
Earth Shoes	Close. But not a flip-flop.	Ah, feet-in-the-grass feeling without getting them dirty.	The Earth is to be developed.
Deck Shoes	Don't laugh. The deck gets slippery.	The no-slip rubber sole gives me all the support I need.	Call me Captain.
Clogs	I've never seen these in Baja.	No backstrap. No thanks.	They do make my legs look longer.
Oxfords	Just hang me.	Well, I am ordering wine with lunch.	I like to dress up my khaki short shorts.
Italian Leather Slides	Not even in Italy.	Comfortable, but not secure.	Of course. I bought them in Milan.
Barefoot	Love the wind in my toes.	Okay, but only for a minute.	Barefoot? I bet you want to know stock secrets too?

Where do your man's playtime shoes land on the Soleology Vulnerability Continuum?

Play

Hangs Loose ⟵⟶ **Can't Let Go**

Open and Free | Comfortable yet Secure | A Modified Loafer

Sole Story

Lucie was a Southern California beach girl at heart. That's why it was very important to her that she met a man who she thought was beach compatible. Yet while living abroad in Rome, she found that was easier said than done. In the city, men were gorgeous by the dozen and their shoes were fabulous. All perfect tens. The leather was supple and fine. The stitching was stylishly superb, and each pair of shoes looked as if it jumped off the cover of Men's Vogue magazine. The Roman city-suit look made Lucie drool. She was afraid to turn her head to check out one guy lest she miss the next gorgeous Roman walking through the piazza. But that was in the city. The everlasting love test was to take them to the beach.

This is where Lucie learned how European men can go so very right but then so very wrong. Marco, an impeccably dressed man sporting stunning loafers with whom she had lunched in the Piazza del Popolo, was strutting down the beach, fine clothing replaced by a bandana tied over his forehead, and white banana hammock. His former exquisite city shoes replaced by a pair of white jelly beach sandals. One look at the jelly sandals and Lucie knew she just couldn't go there. Even when back in Rome, the image of the jellies haunted her and killed off any attraction she was feeling for either Marco or Flavio or Allessandro.

As shocking as the beach was for Lucie, what she learned next was even more shocking. Who was responsible for keeping these Roman gods' suits and shoes looking so fine? Their mothers! Most of the single men well into their thirties still lived with their mothers who not only ironed their shirts but also shined their shoes. Lucie decided that if she was going to "go Euro," they were going to have to win the trifecta. She needed a man who pulled off the city-suit look, passed the beach test, and didn't live with his mother. Only then would he win a date with her.

Archetype Category: Sport
Represents: Competition

Once out of the daily grind, men undergo an amazing transformation while they put on their athletic shoes. As they lace up, hook in, or buckle down, prepare for their inner animal to come out. Sports are a necessary outlet for men to be their gritty selves, sweat, get dirty, and win. It doesn't matter if they play on a tennis court, in a field, or game online, men will compete against anything. It's their nature. Be warned that when a man is wearing his sport shoes, he isn't the sweet guy who brings you coffee in the morning anymore. He's macho, primal, and operating from his caveman survival tendencies.

Three archetypes represent competition: Always on the Mountain, Only on the Field, and Sport Fashion Fantasy. Whichever archetype your man falls into, it gives you an insight into his classic competitive nature. This aspect of competition is important in relationships because men compete against *everything:* man against nature, man against man, and man against self. Yet, if you begin to compete against each other, unless it's a friendly match, the playing field in your relationship can feel more like a battlefield.

COMPETITION ARCHETYPE #1: ALWAYS ON THE MOUNTAIN

You can take the man out of the mountains but not the mountains out of the man. Some men wear Tevas while actually crossing a river. Others wear them shopping for incense on Melrose Ave. Whatever element the shoe represents to an Always on the Mountain Man, he carries it into his everyday experience. An Always on the Mountain Man views the city as a sprawling urban jungle—or garden—filled with intriguing yet potentially dangerous nocturnal and sun-loving beasts. He also has the ability to transform seemingly ordinary activities into an intriguing adventure.

An Always on the Mountain Man loathes the mundane. Observe as he scales stairs, hunts for a parking space, circles high stock indexes, surfs the web, attacks his new workout plan, surveys the bar, and roves the land in his SUV. With every Velcro, buckle, snap, or tie, an Always on the Mountain Man's feet are prepared for anything a *Raiders of the Lost Arc* movie might throw at him. He's been training and he's ready.

The quintessential shoe of the Always on the Mountain Man is the Teva. An open-toed-wraparound ankle-Velcro-hybrid water/land-adventure shoe, men who wear Tevas are making a statement. They say, "I am an outdoorsman. I can go anywhere. Leather does not restrict me." Even when worn in the city, the Teva promise of unlimited adventure helps a man maintain his outdoor status by giving off the air, "I'm in the city, but I am not of it."

Tevas and its contemporaries are considered the ultimate *off-roading freedom shoe*. Yet as always with marketing, imitation is flattery. The demand for the off-roading freedom shoe grew and expanded to the point that it actually stepped on its original freedom idea. Today there are Teva-inspired shoes that you cannot get wet. They are made of leather, which is the very thing that the original brand liberated men from. If you see a man wearing Teva-inspired shoes that step on its original freedom idea, he may not be an Always on the Mountain Man. He could be (gasp!) an amphibious water/-land-adventurer wannabe. Depending on who you want to date—the real deal or a marketing spin-off—the answer you find may be worth a second look.

Definition

The Off-Roading Freedom Shoe—*Any shoe that makes a man feel like he can climb any mountain or cross any river.*

While dating an Always on the Mountain Man, it's unwise to burst his adventure bubble. Instead, play along, especially if it doesn't cost you anything. Besides, you just might like playing his adventure game. Because if you disturb what may or may not be fantasy to him, prepare for a very unhappy and possibly very hurt adventurer. Always on the Mountain men take their adventures very seriously wherever they are. So don't laugh if you see an exaggerated puffing of his chest when another male walks by. He's trying to be your hero and protect you. And why not let him? In these days of Women's Lib and self-sufficiency, men can only be a hero when we let them.

There's a few ways to play along with his adventure game. When an Always on the Mountain Man rushes to open your door, pretend that he just saved you from a pit of venomous snakes. When he walks on the outside of the sidewalk with you to protect you from potential disaster, tell him how safe you feel with such a big strong man. Then feel his big strong muscles. Even if you're a black belt in karate, if you let your Always on the Mountain Man feel like a hero, he'll act like one. Besides, you can never be too careful. It is a jungle out there.

COMPETITION ARCHETYPE #2: ONLY ON THE FIELD

Men who lace up, hook, or buckle down their sport shoes only when they're actually playing a sport tend to concentrate on one thing at a time. Their minds operate something like this: *I'm an animal.* I'm not an animal. *I'm an animal.* I'm not an animal. An Only on the Field kind of guy has a one-track mind. When he's sleeping, he's sleeping. When he's cooking, he's cooking. When he's working, he's working. When he's not, he's not. And that's when you get him. He may also be very practical and compartmentalized or have an exceptionally orderly garage or shoe closet. Don't be surprised if you find a labeler in his kitchen drawer. Only on the Field Men can be quite the organizers.

Typically an Only on the Field Man keeps his shoes just as compartmentalized as his life. Instead of wearing one pair of cross trainers for everything, he will have a distinctly different pair of sport shoes for running, walking, playing tennis or basketball, hiking, and doing any other activity you can think of. This is a man who is driven by performance. He wouldn't think of playing a sport without its corresponding shoes. That would sacrifice his competitive edge. This one also has a high meltdown risk if he can't find what shoes he needs for optimum performance. To avoid a nuclear meltdown, you may want to have a "consolation" pair of backup sport shoes that he can use in a pinch.

Only in the Field Men can be quite handy. Count on them to know the function of every gadget, gizmo, zip, clip, and tie. He prefers shoes that are high tech, perhaps futuristic, and that are on the cutting edge of sport-performance technology. Essentially, his shoes are another "gadget" or a precision instrument in his quiver of performance gear. He'll know exactly what material the Super Flux Extended-Jump Heel Projector Cushion is made of and its direct relationship to the Turbo Support Ultra Breathe Insole. You don't have to be an engineer to date an Only on the Field Man. Yet, it's in your best interest to be understanding when his shoe collection takes up just as much room in the closet as yours.

COMPETITION ARCHETYPE #3: SPORT FASHION FANTASY

Since the 1980s, athletic shoe companies have profited from mega sport heroes endorsing their sneakers. These sneakers not only have reached hero collectable status, have a fan base, have dedicated websites and publications but also have crossed into the realm of Sport Fashion Fantasy. This is achieved when the function of the shoe is totally overlooked. Instead, Sport Fashion Fantasy Men wear them solely for the status of sporting a limited edition label on a $200 sneaker that has never seen the court, freestyle park, or the intended venue. Rather these sport shoes are worn while "kickin' it" (a sport in itself) or playing video games. You can expect Sport Fashion Fantasy Men to dust, clean, and idolize their shoes. Perhaps, even keep them in their original boxes, and they call themselves "sneaker heads." For Sport Fashion Fantasy Men, it's the look and feel of being associated with greatness that counts, instead of shooting for the hoop themselves.

If you're on a date with a man in Sport Fashion Fantasy shoes be careful not to scuff them or let your ice cream drip on the leather. Also, don't expect a Sport Fashion Fantasy Man actually to be in shape. He's not wearing sport shoes to play a sport. Instead, he's playing a part, and unfortunately, that burns more bridges than fat. In fact, the only sport he's interested in playing is a game of catch. Guess what? You're the ball. All that fashion and flash on his foot is really for your eyes only. Before you go dismissing Sport Fashion Fantasy Men, remember who always gets the girl: the hero. Underneath it all, that's what it's really about. You. Sport Fashion Fantasy Men just want to find someone to love. Yet, what they forget is that the hero gets the girl by doing what he does best, which is being himself.

Before you classify his shoes as lame, first find out who endorses his sneakers because most likely that's his hero. And if his hero is a man with qualities you can respect, perhaps it's not so bad that your Sports Fashion Fantasy Man wants to be more like him. Everyone starts somewhere. And with you by his side, perhaps your Sports Fashion Fantasy Man may feel more like a hero himself and feel less inclined to walk in another man's shoes.

That's one side of the Sport Fashion Fantasy story. Here's the flip side. Although, the rage first started with basketball shoes endorsed by NBA heroes, it didn't stop there. The surf/skate/snow industry got its foot in the door by sponsoring "alternative" or indie athletes. Indie athletes have a mantra: fellowship, not followship, and compete in extreme sports featured on the X-Games. Old-school sneaker companies associated with the indie athlete have become cultural icons of self-expression. So much that Vans, one of the original skateboard shoe companies, has the slogan "I am an individual."

Beyond the indie athlete, the greater creative community has embraced Converse sneakers as a symbol of the relentless pursuit of self-expression. Now, it doesn't matter if you see a man wearing an Armani suit or Levi's jeans when walking down the street. If he's wearing a pair of bright red Converse sneakers, he might as well hang a sign over his feet saying "I'm artistic!" These types of shoes are extremely popular among graphic artists where self-expression has become a sport in itself. They use not only pictures but also their shoe choice to convey their message to the world.

Whether it's basketball or the surf/skate/snow industry, Sport Fashion Fantasy can go both ways. It just depends on his intention behind wearing the shoes. It makes a difference in the man when he's wearing these shoes either to be more like someone else or to express more of himself. To discern the difference between the two, your sole impression has all the right moves.

Like fantasy sports cars, streetwear sneakers are usually lime green, fire engine red, or Lamborghini yellow with some

Arrested Development: Streetwear Sneaker Men

It's not far-fetched to compare men's collectable streetwear sneakers to boys' collectable toys. In fact, the two have more in common than not. The evolution of boys' toys goes something like this: Boys play with fast little red sports cars. Then they go to school and work hard so as adults they can buy fast little red sports cars. But if a man can't afford the adult 3-D version of his boyhood fantasy car, he can at least wear fast shoes on his feet.

Boys' Fantasy Cars	***Men's Fantasy Sneakers***
Gadgets	Gadgets
Gizmos	Gizmos
Air pumps	Air pumps
High tech	High tech
Supersonic special powers	Supersonic special powers
Endorsed by a superhero	Endorsed by a superhero
Limited edition	Limited edition
Club memberships	Club memberships
Collectable	Collectable
Idolized	Idolized
Fan base	Fan base

"fast" line design that has a graffiti artist's edge. Although you might not hear them coming, when you see them, they certainly make some noise. Since streetwear sneaker men loath limitation and are in a high pursuit of self-expression, they have developed a certain lingo that makes you part of the klub. Most *c*'s are replaced with a *k* and there are lots of extra *z*'s. For example, "I juz want to say that my new kickz (sneakers) are the shizzle cuz they are out of tha box kool and kickin'." Also, prepare for a major bling thing going on. Diamonds are now a street sneaker's best friend, making them a little more klassy. On a Saturday night, men can juice up their sneakers with diamond-studded shoelace clips. Ask him: Are those diamonds on your shoes? Or are you just happy to see me? Or if he's just a friend, knock knuckles and tell him "sweet laces, keep 'em loose."

Sole Story

When Esmé started a new job at a vitamin company, she became a bit wary when she discovered that her boss wore Sport Fashion Fantasy footwear. Every day he sported a pair of pristine Air Jordans or their flashy equivalent. Her boss Jack commonly cornered her in her cubicle until she commented on his shoes and told him how cool they were. Jack would constantly fuss over them, wiping off a scuff, and he had a growing collection of leather protection products on his desk. He also had a Polaroid of himself surrounded by his Sport Fashion Fantasy shoes fanned out like a flower.

It wasn't until Esmé met up with a girlfriend after work that she realized the full extent of her boss's affinity for boyhood collectables. As she began describing her new boss, Esmé's girlfriend burst out laughing. "I know that guy," she said, "I met him online." Evidently Jack had a permanent ad for a "roommate" on a community website and preferred "females only." Esmé's friend told her how he wouldn't stop talking about his shoe collection, which at first she thought was kind of cool because she was into shoes as well.

Yet, the roommate situation was a total no-go when Jack invited her over to check out his apartment. Not only did he collect Sport Fashion Fantasy shoes, but he also collected toys. Lining the mirrored walls of his apartment were hundreds of superhero toys all in their original boxes. It didn't take a minute to realize that this was no roommate situation. The next day Esmé requested to be transferred to a different department. She was glad she did. Three weeks later Jack was fired for what was politely described as "disruption." Evidently, he was more into his shoes than his job.

HOW TO SPOT AN ONLY ON THE FIELD OR ALWAYS ON THE MOUNTAIN OR SPORT FASHION FANTASY MAN

Test your sole impressions. Match the archetypes for sport expressed by the different attitudes attached to the shoes.

ARCHETYPES

	Only on the Field	Always on the Mountain	Sport Fashion Fantasy
The shoes	*Attitudes toward them*		
White Sneakers	Only at the gym.	I go everywhere in comfort and performance.	*Miami Vice* lives! Nothing looks better with my peach suit.
Air Jordans	I really do jump higher.	All I need is a hoop.	They look great with my acid-wash jeans.
Bike Shoes	Only because I have to. And don't look at my legs.	I love the sound of plastic clacking on the floor.	I look hot in a yellow jersey. And my legs are really smooth.
Hiking Boots	Yes, I climb mountains.	Can't you tell I I climb mountains?	I knew someone who climbed mountains, and he looked like this.
Tevas	When the rivers run.	I live in Seattle. The rivers always run.	Don't I look sporty? And the Velcro is fun to play with.

	Only on the Field	Always on the Mountain	Sport Fashion Fantasy
The shoes	*Attitudes toward them*		
Ski Boots	Get these damn things off.	I like to walk with them over my shoulder.	I know it's 2 A.M. I'm an après-ski dancing machine!
Urban Hybrid City Hikers	I take a walk at lunch.	Carpet is a low savanna.	Chicks dig the guy in the ad for Sport Fashion Fantasy City Hikers.
Slip-on Nylon Amphibious Water Booties	I free dive off a rocky shore.	Everywhere I go is a rocky shore.	They matched my yellow snorkel at the Sandals Resort.
Rollerblades	I'm pro.	I joined a city club.	I've got the fluorescent t-back tank top to match.
Golf Shoes	Just sealed a deal on the 18th hole.	Shhh. I'm golfing.	Where's the 19th hole?

Where do your man's shoes land on the Soleology Sport Continuum?

The Soleology Sport Continuum

An Animal ⟷ **Wants to Be an Animal**

Always on the Mountain	Only on the Field	Sport Fashion Fantasy

The Sneaker Bonus Pages

The sneaker has become a part of the American man experience, just as much as beer and football. Just like there are hundreds of types of pasta in Italy—there are hundreds of sneakers to choose from in America. The choices may be mind-boggling, but there are a few that stand out.

THE UBIQUITOUS WHITE SNEAKER: THE NONCOMMUNICATOR

As much as shoes talk, there's one that doesn't. And what it doesn't say is what speaks the loudest. When men don the Ubiquitous White Sneaker, they're flying under the communication radar screen. Perhaps this is why these shoes are so ubiquitous. As far as men's footwear goes, they're the lowest common denominator. Although they're technically considered a sneaker, it's difficult to call it a sport shoe because they're rarely worn for any particular sport. Instead, they're worn for all occasions—*both* on and off the couch.

The most common argument for the Ubiquitous White Sneaker is that they're comfortable. Yet, the lowest common denominator usually is. The Ubiquitous White Sneaker adds about as much flavor to a man as mayonnaise spices up a sandwich. Generally, you find them coupled with a cotton XL T-shirt with a free advertisement printed on the back for a product he doesn't care much about either. In such a case, it's clear that the Ubiquitous White Sneaker Man is someone who's shut himself off from *the shoe aspect of life*. Once the communication valve is shut off in one area of a man's life, it's usually blocked in other areas as well. When nothing is flowing, it's difficult for anything to trickle down. Men who don't communicate with their shoes usually have difficulty communicating within themselves and among others. It's important to ask yourself that if your man isn't participating in the shoe aspect of life, where else is he operating under the radar?

Definition

The Shoe Aspect of Life—*Our deepest essence of self that we express through our choice in shoes.*

Whether discussing life or shoes, it's true that for every action there's an equal and opposite reaction. Ubiquitous White Sneakers are so remarkably uncommunicative that urban shoe companies popular with revolutionary pop artists and underground musicians have taken the Ubiquitous White Sneaker, turned it on its head, and made a statement out of its nonstatement. Revolutionary White Sneaker men wear the antithesis of the Ubiquitous White Sneaker by adding a splash of neon or metallic as a protest against everyone who won't. They took what used to fly under the communication radar and made it say something. Revolutionary White Sneaker men are committed to be the voice of all that isn't "comfortable," which, this time *around*, says a lot.

Where does your man's sneakers land on the Communication Radar Scale?

Communication Radar Scale

Uncommunicative ⟵⟶ Communicative

DR. SOLE

Q. *Help! I'm living with a noncommunicating White Ubiquitous Sneaker Man. I love him, but I can't take it anymore. What do I do?*

A. The first action you can take to spark communication is to hide the TV remote. At least he will ask you where you put it. But seriously, a man who has cut himself off from his shoe aspect of life has usually cut himself off from other aspects of life as well. While approaching this matter, it's best to be gentle and compassionate—because somewhere, something happened that made him snap shut like a giant clam.

Perhaps he used to try to communicate through his shoes, but after some traumatic experience with the wrong shoes, he decided never again to be vulnerable that way. If this is the case, let him know that it's safe to communicate with his shoes without being criticized or laughed at. Try at least for a day to listen to everything he says without judgment. Then watch him open up like a flower. He'll begin to communicate again in small subtle ways. Encourage him. Keep up the compassion and nonjudgment. Soon you'll see that his behavior will change. Eventually, he will actually want to communicate again with his shoes, and you'll see less and less of the Ubiquitous White Sneakers on his feet. That is, of course, unless he is just plain lazy—which is an entirely different can of worms. □

Sole Story

Gina met a producer at a trendy bar in Los Angeles. In the first two minutes of their conversation, he flashed a wad of hundreds followed by the claim that he could buy the place in cash. Yet, when Gina looked at his shoes, she noticed a pair of cheap Velcro-secure top Ubiquitous White Sneakers. Casually, Gina asked the producer where he bought his shoes. He answered with enthusiasm, "Costco! They were so cheap I bought four pairs!" Gina asked, "But do you like them?" "No," he answered, "but they're really comfortable."

It would have been a different sole story if he had answered that he loved these shoes so much he bought four pairs. But he didn't. Instead, the producer got nervous and started flashing his wad of cash again hoping Gina wouldn't notice that regardless of how much money he had what he felt most comfortable in was what he didn't like.

THE UBIQUITOUS BLACK SNEAKER

The kissing cousin of the Ubiquitous White Sneaker is the Ubiquitous Black Sneaker. Popular among engineers and scientists, these shoes don't say much other than, "I'm really good at math." Yet, when it comes to dating someone who is really good at math, special rules apply. Scientists and engineers have a system for everything whether it's calculating the trajectory of a satellite, developing a molecular superstructure, or optimizing the loading space of your dishwasher. It's very painful for a Ubiquitous Black Sneaker Man to see you employing less than scientifically proven methods for your personal organization. Although incredibly annoying, teaching you how to develop a superior system to maximize your personal habits really is an act of love. All Ubiquitous Black Sneaker men really want is for you to enjoy the increased time, speed, and space their engineering endeavors can give you.

Another special rule that applies to Ubiquitous Black Sneaker men is that they usually lack the sensitivity gene. Don't expect them to understand when you tell them to buzz off because you just don't "feel" like working to your optimum space/time capacity. All they see is the wasted potential of what could have been if you only had "felt" like getting up off the couch.

If you spin it right, the perk for dating a Ubiquitous Black Sneaker Man can be quite an adventure. Since many of them have high-level security clearances, it could be the closest you'll get to being a Bond Girl. Yet, if you like him but are having trouble getting over his shoes, there's a quick fix that can satisfy you both. Rather than him exposing himself as a target for unscrupulous covert international organizations, you might convince him to go *undercover* and wear shoes that say, "I'm really bad at math." Tell him you'll sleep better at night knowing that your man is doing all he can to protect the safety of our country.

Alternative Footwear Options for the Numerical Genius

Here are a few options for Ubiquitous Black Sneaker men who are willing to trade in their traditional taste in footwear to go undercover as to not expose their scientific genius and jeopardize our homeland security. While these shoes don't mean that the men who wear them are necessarily bad at math, they certainly don't advertise, "I'm really good at math" either.

- "Street Smart" sneakers
- Zips
- Espadrilles
- Roughrider motorcycle boots
- Flip-flops, slaps, sandals, or slides
- Anything made from hemp

Archetype Category: Fantasy
Represents: Escape

We all like to get away and escape from our daily grind. That's why we go to the movies and love a happy ending. Or we may escape to a tropical destination, lose our self inside a book, go to a costume party, or put on a pair of blue suede shoes. Whether it's for a night, a week, or forever, the shoes a man puts on his feet help him live out his escape fantasy. Whatever type of escape your man is looking for, his shoes are his ticket to ride. There are three archetypes that represent the different aspects of escape. Behind door number one, two, and three are Just for Tonight, I Think I Like It Here, and Blast Off!.

While discovering what type of escape artist you are dealing with, it's important to note the frequency of his trips to Fantasy Island. Some men like to leave themselves behind for a day or a night. Like a trip to Vegas, they don't want to stay too long. Some extend their stay and buy a time-share. While others take up permanent residence and never leave. Even if his feet are still on the ground, the right pair of shoes can make your man feel like he's orbiting in outer space. Wherever your man decides to travel, make sure that his shoes are ticketed to return. That is, of course, if you want to see him again.

Oh, you *do* want to see him again. So, when it comes to his fantasy escape tendencies, don't scoff when your middle-management escape artist suddenly comes home with a pair of roughed up motorcycle boots. Don't ask, "What are *these* for?" You know what they're for. He bought them to escape and get away. Remember that some amount of fantasy is a natural and necessary part of our lives. Just about every woman has shoes in her closet that she can barely walk in and will probably never wear. Yet, the idea of having them is more important than actually wearing them.

So, be a doll and give your Rocket Man a hall pass to the moon for an *outer-shoe experience*. Give him the space he needs to feel like the cool guy in *Easy Rider*, a rock star, or whatever star he's reaching for. And if you do feel like laughing, look in the mirror first. Make sure it isn't you who he's escaping from.

Definition

Outer-Shoe Experience—*The immediate effect a pair of shoes has on a man to transport him to a different dimension of himself.*

ESCAPE ARCHETYPE #1: JUST FOR TONIGHT

Escape is a natural thing, and traditionally society gives us a few nights off a year. Take Halloween for example. It's a public permission slip to be totally ridiculous, embarrassing, suave, or slutty. Carnaval and Mardi Gras give us the nod for a whole weekend of debauchery and shakin' it. And if you need a few extra nights off, throw a seventies party, buy your man a pair of snakeskin zip-up ankle boots, and let him feel like a pimp for a night.

Yet if you find that your arms are still crossed, consider the saying "All work and no play make Jack a dull boy." The same goes for relationships. One of the advantages of being with a Just for Tonight escape artist is that you can escape together. There's no longevity or commitment. It doesn't have to mean anything or have any impact on your future together. It can be sheer whim and whimsy. After all, it's just for tonight. Play along if you think it's a game you'll enjoy and feel comfortable playing. Yet remember who to beam him back home to or keep your return tickets tucked tightly in your purse.

And if your man does decide to include you in his escapes, remember that no matter how ridiculous he looks, dances, or acts—if you let him enjoy his escape, most likely he'll wake up refreshed and secretly grateful in the morning. When you let a man be who he is—even if it's a very bad dancer in even worse secondhand disco shoes—you may find that it amplifies all those other qualities you love about him even more.

Also, don't think life has to get crazy for a Just for Tonight Man to escape. If you're dating a penny loafer penny-pincher, he may get a wild hair, throw on his "good" shoes, spend a dime, and take you out for a night of romance. But if the night does get off the hook, remember that there's a difference between going to see the show and driving home with the band. The metallic patent leather shoes and bling come off before he goes to sleep, and you wake up to see the same man you knew and loved the night before. Otherwise, he's not a Just for Tonight kind of guy. Instead, he's well on his way to the next fantasy archetype: I Think I Like It Here.

ESCAPE ARCHETYPE #2: I THINK I LIKE IT HERE

This guy is similar to your Yes, Sir! archetype, except he has a dream. Rocket Man just took a trip last night to outer space, and he liked it so much that he secured a temporary visa. He's dibble dabbling, wavering back and forth. Should I shoot for Mars? Or return to Earth? His hand is hovering above the warp speed button, and he's thinking about making it so. Perhaps by day he's the morning manager of your local grocery store. But every Thursday night he rocks out as Jimmy Hendrix in a cover band. I Think I like It Here guys are the real middle men. They desire to live out their fantasy but haven't made the commitment to do it full time.

An I Think I Like It Here guy embraces the "work to live" philosophy, which usually makes it very easy for you to differentiate between his work shoes and his shoes that are a part of his fantasy footwear collection. His fantasy shoes will be kept separate from his work shoes. Perhaps even set apart like a showpiece. They will be flashy by nature, with more flair and style than he could ever get away with at his day job. They might have gothic studs, white leather, heavy buckles and straps, gold laces, exotic animal skin, exaggerated heels—anything that doesn't say, "I work in a cubicle."

If your man's fantasy footwear collection is prominently displayed (while his work shoes are tossed to the back), then he wants you to know him for who he is *really*, not how he pays the bills. Yet if you discover his Western country-crooner boots tucked away in the back, he's not ready to come out of the "fantasy footwear" closet.

If kept in balance, I Think I Like It Here Man can be quite fun. You can make out with Jimmy Hendrix backstage every Thursday night and become his biggest fan. Yet if left unbalanced and unchecked and if he feels like he's *wandering* in outer space, "Jimmy" can easily become resentful toward both his day job and his real job because neither one is fully satisfying. Ask yourself and ask him what aspect of his life does he identify with more. Working toward his dreams or working to pay the bills? The answer is an important indication of what trickles are coming your way in your relationship with him.

ESCAPE ARCHETYPE #3: BLAST OFF!

Talk about commitment! Blast Off! Man is going for the dream. He's hit warp speed, and isn't looking back, which can usually go either one of two ways: (1) He was never meant to be the morning manager of your local grocery store, and he's destined to be the greatest Jimmy Hendrix cover-band lounge singer that ever existed. (2) He really was meant to be the morning manager of your grocery store, and he's running from his destiny by dressing up every Thursday night as Jimmy Hendrix and trying to fill his shoes.

Just like our morning manager running from his destiny, some people would rather be anyone but themselves. If your Rocket Man suddenly fancies himself a rapper, cowboy, pimp, bard, gangster, aviator, surfer, or road warrior, it's important to ask two questions:

1. Has he discovered a new aspect of himself that you can support him in exploring?
2. Or is he a *poser?*

Posers come in a variety of shapes and sizes and shoes. There are "rockers" in Los Angeles who have never played in a band. There are "cowboys" who have never ridden a horse. Posers take on a look. Nothing more. And their shoes help them get there.

The biggest tip-off when dealing with a poser is that his fantasy shoes will be brand spanking new or hardly have a scuff on them. Most men who are actually living their fantasy lives live and work in these shoes. So much that they are usually in "used" or ratty condition. A real rocker is all over the stage working it, kicking, jumping, and breaking guitars. And a real cowboy is ankle deep in mud among other things, which can take a toll on the sparkle and suede of his new cowboy boots.

If you can see your reflection in your man's fantasy shoes, most likely he is a poser and his shoes are *poser props.* Since all things trickle down, make sure he isn't using you as a prop too. If you're enjoying your man's sudden transformation—fabulous! Go with it. If not, Nancy Sinatra knows some boots that were made for walking.

Definitions

Poser—*A most unconvincing magician whose act is all smoke and broken mirrors.*

Poser Props—*The physical frills of a poser's smoke and broken mirrors act meant to distract you from the truth.*

Poser Checklist

Your man has achieved official poser status if he does the following:

- Suddenly wants to be referred to as Captain, Daddy, or Chief.
- Considers you lucky to be hanging out with him.
- Treats you like a groupie instead of a girlfriend.
- Keeps all poser props generally unused out-of-the-box new.
- Becomes unnecessarily upset or inconsolable if any poser props are damaged, lost, or stepped on.
- Has "his people" return your calls.

HOW TO SPOT A JUST FOR TONIGHT OR I THINK I LIKE IT HERE OR BLAST OFF! MAN

Test your sole impressions. Match the Soleology archetypes for Fantasy expressed by the different attitudes attached to the shoes.

ARCHETYPES

	Just for Tonight	I Think I Like It Here	Blast Off!
The shoes	*Attitudes toward them*		
Exotic Animal-Print Booties	Kinda cool—for five bucks.	Bought the matching exotic-print sheets.	Hear me roar, baby!
Blue Suede Shoes	My hips hurt from rockin'.	Whatever Elvis can do, I can do better.	Hit the Miami Beach senior circuit.
Motorcycle Boots	Dig the shoes.	Bought a Harley.	Knocked out my teeth, and showering is for sissies.
Cowboy Boots	Wednesday night free two-stepping lessons.	Bought the Wranglers too.	Paid $1,000 to haul horseshit on a ranch for a week.
Crocodile-Skin Pimp Daddies	Another Pimp 'n' Ho Party.	Low riding the Boulevard.	Moved to Vegas and opened a dude ranch. No, the other kind.
White Leather Disco King Loafers	Rented *Saturday Night Fever.*	Hung a disco ball in my living room.	Bought a disco.

	Just for Tonight	I Think I Like It Here	Blast Off!
The shoes	*Attitudes toward them*		
Basketball Shoes	High five at the H.S. reunion.	Wanna look at my yearbook?	I was team captain in 1973.
Combat Boots	I'm a soldier for Halloween.	Heat vision goggles and camouflage.	Reported for duty.
Scarpa Ski Boots	Signed up for a ½-day back-country ski tour.	I wonder if I can tele-commute from Vail.	Went feral, live in an igloo, and poach ski runs.
White Huaraches	3-day, 4-night package tour to Acapulco.	Another margarita please!	Me llamo Jose. No hablo ingles.
Teva Travelers	Full moon party in Thailand.	Thai pants and sarong skirts.	Fathered communal eco-community on secret idyllic beach.

Where do your man's shoes land on the Soleology Fantasy Continuum?

The Soleology Escape Continuum

Ticketed for Return ⟵⟶ ***Full Speed Ahead***

Just for Tonight	I Think I Like It Here	Blast Off!

Generation H—Hybrids: Dress Me Up. Dress Me Down.

Just like Chaka Kahn's 1970s hit "I'm Every Woman," today there is a shoe for every man. It's called the Hybrid. Hybrids offer men more choices to express themselves through their shoes because they create a gray area between Work, Play, Sport, and Fantasy footwear. Shoe companies are taking the conservative lines of the traditional dress shoe, bending them, and adding the comfort and performance of a sneaker. They've also dressed up the sneaker by adding the conservative lines of a traditional dress shoe. It's hard to tell where the hiking boot ends and the hipster bowler begins. You can even find "Mullet" open-heel dress shoes. It's business in the front and a party in the back.

Generation H men are usually forward thinkers and don't like to be pegged into any category, which is why their shoes straddle the fence. They generally enjoy alternate lifestyles and progressive ways of living. They are the pioneers of change and want to wear shoes that reflect who they are and what they stand for. Their footwear can include vegan shoes that walk as gently on the earth as they do or an integrative design that allows them to go more places than ever before.

The only drawback with hybrids is that they come in three

shapes: the good, the bad, and the fugly. A shoe whose aim is purely function can end up looking really, really weird. Yet sometimes the weird factor becomes a form of expression in itself and explains why hybrid shoes are quite popular among artists. It's not just life anymore but also shoes that imitate art.

Putting It All Together: Your Man's Archetype at a Glance

To answer *Pre*relationship Question #1: Who is he really? put an X where he lands on each of the Soleology *Arch*etype Continuums. Now, you can see him from all different angles in his relationship to Authority, Play, Sport, and Fantasy.

Authority Continuum

Play Continuum

Hangs Loose ⟷ ***Can't Let Go***

Open and Free	Comfortable yet Secure	A Modified Loafer

Sport Continuum

An Animal ⟷ ***Wants to Be an Animal***

Always on the Mountain	Only on the Field	Sport Fashion Fantasy

Escape Continuum

Ticketed for Return ⟷ ***Full Speed Ahead***

Just for Tonight	I Think I Like It Here	Blast Off!

Now that you know more about your potential future loverman—what about you? What is your relationship to Work, Play, Sport, and Fantasy? Do you like to doll up just for Halloween? Or do you have a permanent gig as geisha girl hostess at a Japanese restaurant? Perhaps you love the smell of Monday in the morning and you can't wait to wear your power pumps at the office? Or would nothing make you happier than sliding your toes into a fluffy pair of pink bunny slippers? The point of learning more about men isn't to see how you'll fit into their lives, but to know what they're going to add to yours! Understanding a man's Archetypical implications is the first step to decide if his shoes fit not only his feet but also the romantic relationship of your dreams.

Close your eyes and imagine your shoes living side by side his in the same closet. Is there a spark? Can you see your shoes getting along? Are they moving in closer for a smooch or, perhaps, a flirtatious nudge? Or are they inching away, as you start to squirm, and you're not quite sure what to do? The answers to these questions and to Pre-Relationship Question #2: How does he feel about himself, *really?* in the next chapter will help you calculate your Solemate Compatibility Factor before you invest not only your time in a relationship but also your heart.

CHAPTER 6

Sole Profiling

Sole Quote:

"There's an awful lot you could tell about a person by their shoes. Where they're going. Where they've been . . . " —Forrest Gump

Both men and women put up a good front. *Think about it:* how often do we actually tell the truth when someone asks us how we're feeling? Perhaps, we respond with the perfunctory "I'm fine" because we think the person asking doesn't really want to know, which, of course, they usually don't. Yet, what's a girl to do when she really wants to know how a man is feeling, especially about himself? Simply, conduct a little sole reconnaissance, the ultimate in-the-field exercise. Understanding how a man feels about himself is very important. It can make the difference between kissing a prince or kissing a prince who unfortunately thinks he's a frog.

For best-case scenario sole reconnaissance, make sure you have access to your man's closet where you can not only see all his shoes at a glance but also take a sampling of the quality of life his shoes experience. Many ways are available to do this without raising any unnecessary suspicion. One fun and unassuming way to gain access to a man's closet is to ask him if you can pick out his shoes. Tell him it's just as hot as putting on his tie or the *new* foreplay. Say whatever it takes—just get your nose in his closet. Another option is simply to go for it. Swing open his closet doors and say, "Let's see your shoes!"

A man with nothing to hide will take you on a tour of his fancy footwear collection. But if there's a skeleton in his shoe closet, he'll scurry you away with some excuse about the kitchen being more interesting (or clean) while trying to divert your *sole profiling* efforts. Take note of his reactions. How open or closed a man is about revealing his shoes is directly proportional to how open or closed he is about revealing himself.

Definition

Sole Profile—*The big picture you put together about a man that determines his dateability through various methods of Awareness Expansion.*

It's also wise to take random samplings. Perhaps he already knows that your nose will be in his closet and he has cleaned up for your special night. Check back later to see if there are any major changes in the quality of life his shoes experience in his closet. Three random samplings without prior notification should do the trick. Also, FYI: anytime you arrive unannounced at a man's house, it's wise to come bearing hot pizza or cold beer or both.

Your Zoom Lens

While conducting sole reconnaissance, let your eyes zoom in and out like a camera to gain both the wide-angle and close-up perspective of his shoes. This is important because on closer inspection, your zoom lens may have picked up something that your wide-angle shot missed. Photographers know that the devil is in the details. It may be one detail of his shoes—a tassel or the stitching—that makes you give the *secret signal* to your friends to come and save you. In contrast, if you take in only the wide-angle perspective, it can prompt a different signal from you to give him a come hither over-the-shoulder hair toss as you inch in closer and close the gap.

Definition

Secret Signal—*A gesture that appears to be commonplace, such as scratching an itch. Yet to your friends it means "Get your tush over here and save me from this nob!"*

Today your zoom lens is even more important than a wide-angle scan because with fickle fashion trends, it's hard to tell if a man is fashion forward or just broke. For example, the "worn in" or distressed look where shoes out of the box new already look like they've been though the ringer can be particularly misleading. His shoes may make him appear dirt poor, but it's actually a very expensive look, costing twice as much as their look-like-new counterparts. When it comes to shoe talk, these shoes say, "I'm so rich I can buy shoes that already need to be thrown away." But when a man who hasn't two dimes to rub together also wears shoes that look like they've been through the ringer—it may be difficult to tell the difference. Unless of course, if you zoom in. The worn-in-look shoes are usually impeccably clean, while worn-out shoes are usually filthy or quite odorous.

As you adjust your zoom, take note of the following things:

Worn In	***Worn Out***
Expensive	Perhaps were expensive—ten years ago
Shabby Chic	Shabby
Found in Fred Segal	Found on the street
Style Points	Points Deducted
Relaxed	Unraveled
Cares	Careless

One way to conduct quick zoom lens Sole reconnaissance on a date is to pretend that you suddenly lost your contact. Or if you don't wear contacts, lose an earring. And if you don't wear earrings, "accidentally" drop a fork at dinner. While you're on the ground looking for your contact, earring, or fork, you can conveniently check out his shoes.

Regardless of what your zoom lens discovers, remember that Soleology is a *guilt-free zone*. Even if your sole reconnaissance picks up on "*just* one little thing"—a buckle, tassel, or green checkerboard fabric that makes your mouth pucker—or even if one little thread makes you wince, it's important for you to listen to what that thread is saying. It could be only one aspect of a man's shoes that is unappealing, but to you it can feel like a hair in milk or a fly in your soup. It's okay because listening to your self is never being weird or superficial. Besides, there's certainly no shortage of milk, soup, or men.

Sole Story

Jane settled comfortably into her chair at the coffee shop inside her favorite bookstore. Only a few moments later, a handsome man sat next to her and began reading a very sophisticated business book on entrepreneurs. Jane completed the scan, but she could only check him out from the waist up. His feet were tucked under the table. Nonetheless, he was clean shaven, wore a handsome cable-knit sweater, and Jane really appreciated the financial implications of the book he was reading.

Jane's mind started to wander a million miles a second. Suddenly, they were married. He was a successful entrepreneur, her credit card bills were paid off, and she worked two days a week just for fun. Yet as soon as Jane got up the nerve to start a conversation, her future-successful-entrepreneur husband began to fidget and to nervously eye the room. Then he got up abruptly and walked away. Jane caught the weirdo vibe and her eyes instinctively headed south. There they were—a disastrous pair of filthy sneakers that were unraveling and falling apart with the sole flopping about.

In a flash, Jane's hopes of her ex-future husband paying off her credit card debt had been dashed. But Jane was more than grateful for the sole truth. For the next half hour, the guy with the floppy soles got up and sat back down no less than six times. Each time he returned, he had another business book tucked under his arm, which he "read" for less than a minute before walking off again. Jane got up from her table and walked to the register to buy the book she was reading: The Single Girl's Guide to Paying Off Debt.

Definitions

The Scan—*The innate ability of a woman instantly to examine a man from head to toe while picking up signs of whether he could be the father of their children.*

Ex-Future Husband—*Men who we immediately see ourselves married to until we Sole Profile them, and instantly divorce them from our fantasy future.*

Ways to Build His Sole Profile

The point of sole reconnaissance is to build your man's sole profile so that you can discover how he feels about himself. To do this, you want to be hyperaware of certain aspects of a man's shoes and his habits toward them. As the old saying goes, "You can only love someone else as much as you love yourself." If he loves his shoes, that's a really good sign of how much he loves himself—and how much potential love he can lavish onto you!

Sole profiling a man is like putting Windex on glass. You'll be able to see how he feels about himself very clearly. Just like a fingerprint, the information you lift from a man's shoes will give you all the information you need to build his sole profile.

Definition

Sole Profiling—*The art of piecing together your man's inner character based on the outer character of his shoes.*

What to Look For

The speed with which you can build a man's sole profile is based on whether you have access to his closet or just a single pair of shoes. Ideally, you'd have access to his closet right away, but since first dates usually don't begin in his bedroom (although they may end there), it's best to start with a single pair of shoes.

The first step in building your sole profile is to take note of your sole impression. Different elements of his shoes reflect different elements of his personality. In fact, while looking at a man's shoes, they may connote different feelings to you about how he feels about himself. For instance, suede might connote to you a different feeling about his shoes than say purple alligator skin or black pleather. And Astrobright colors on a sneaker certainly give off a different vibe than say, beige.

QUICK CONNOTATIONS

Here's a quick list of connotations you may experience between the physical elements of his shoes and the aspects of his personality that they represent:

Material

Suede	gentleness, natural, vulnerability
Leather	renewable, long-lasting
Nylon	modern, industrial, light, sporty

Stiffness	distance, rigidity
Plastic	modern, urban, edgy

Entry

Slip-on	easygoing, casual
Laces	traditional, youthful
Velcro	security, quick release, rough and prickly
Zipper	retro, feminine
Elastic	relaxed, modern, futuristic

Shape

Narrow	velocity
Boxy	protection
Wide	stability
Long	feminine, sexy
Square	blunt, cutoff, stylistic
Round	smooth, even, and flow

Heel

Wood	square, boxy, traditional
Integrated	smooth, transitional, modern
Rubber	bounce, resilience, playful
Sharp	edgy, cynical, defensive

Sole Relativity

While Soleology is the great decoder, the one doing the decoding is you. The accuracy of Soleology depends not only on your man's shoes but also on how you interpret the situation. To help illustrate this point, consider Soleology's Theory of Relativity:

$S = (NX)^2$
N = His Shoes
X = The Circumstance
Square the product of N and X by your interpretation of his shoes in the circumstance.
S = Your Soleological Relativity Factor

This kind of math is easy because you don't have to check the back of the book to see if you got the answer right. In Soleology, every answer is right because it's yours. But you do have to show your work so that you know how you got your answer. Simply, plug in each value, and the answer you come up with is your own personal Soleological Relativity Factor.

Definition

Soleological Relativity Factor—*What a man's shoes mean* to you.

For you literal literati who prefer a word problem, this one is for you:

1. *The Setup:* your new boyfriend is meeting your parents for the first time for dinner at the best restaurant in town.
2. *The Shoes:* Birkenstocks.
3. The Relativity Factor:

   A. Your parents are hippies who live in Bend, Oregon. They sent your boyfriend Birkenstocks for Christmas. Your man is a hotshot New York lawyer. He *hates* Birkenstocks, but he's wearing them because he knows it'll make your parents happy.

   B. Your parents are prominent hotshot New York lawyers. Your boyfriend is a hippie from Bend, Oregon. He refuses to wear anything but Birkenstocks to dinner—even to The Russian Tea Room.

The Result: The circumstances are the same: dinner with your parents in Birkenstocks. Which is right? Which is wrong? You decide. What's important is the intention behind the shoes he's wearing and the way you perceive the situation. The beauty of Soleological Relativity is that it's in the eye of the beholder—*and that's you.*

Sole Profiling: Man or Boy?

All men have an image of themselves that they want to project and keep until sometime long after it's time for a new one. Although forty is the new thirty, some men like to dress as if they're still in their twenties. The opposite happens when boys in their twenties think and dress like they're in their fifties.

Men's shoes are designed and marketed to a certain age demographic. When men cross over or blur those lines, the message is clear. He's either hanging on to the past or trying to wriggle out of the future, which isn't necessarily a good or bad thing. Except if you think it looks silly when an older man picks you up for a date wearing Eminem's latest and greatest and spewing slang that even you don't know. Don't be surprised when he doesn't understand why you are upset when he says you look *phat* in your new jeans.

As a rule of thumb, Astrobrights; fuzzy textures; elastic laces; images of dragons, ninjas, and graffiti art; the urban London look, or anything punk rock are generally reserved for the young. While neutral colors attached to a more classic, albeit laid-back, design are usually for the more mature young or young at heart. It's interesting to see how as men get older their shoes tend to lose all color until they've morphed into a cushy white orthopedic marshmallow. So if you see an older man wearing Astrobright colors, he's either childish or childlike. Rest assured, your sole impression will pick up on the difference.

On the flip side, it's rare that you'll see a hot guy in his early twenties wearing white orthopedic marshmallows. If you do, this is an old man living in a young gun's body. Or if he's a rebel archetype, perhaps he's wearing them to make a snarky social comment or pulling off the uncool by making it cool again. Snowboarders typically are notorious for recycling old, outdated, or overused looks, turning them on their heads, and making them hip again.

Condition of His Sole

Another way to discover how a man feels about himself is to take careful note of the condition of his shoes. How a man takes care of himself is how he takes care of his shoes. And how a man takes care of his shoes inevitably trickles down onto how he will take care of you. If your man's shoes are well cared for, shiny and polished, ask yourself, where is he well cared for, shiny, and polished? And if his shoes are worn down, broken, unraveling, falling apart, cracked, or blown out, where is he worn down, broken, unraveling, falling apart, cracked, or blown out? You may be surprised how similar your answers are between the two because a man who isn't taking care of his shoes usually isn't taking care of himself in just the same way.

What is the condition of your man's shoes?

New	Broken	Falling apart
Shiny	Worn in	Cracked
Polished	Worn down	Blown out
Well cared for	Unraveling	Other

Now, describe your man's condition. It's no coincidence if the two are surprisingly similar.

Socks and Shoes: Discover What's Under There

While completing your sole reconnaissance, you also want to ask your man to lift a pant leg to discover what lives *under there*. Don't make the mistake of letting this opportunity pass you by. Socks are an extension of his shoes and not only complement but also complete his sole profile. Just like putting your nose in a man's closet, checking out his socks is the second-best way to see if he's got nothing to hide. The discovery of what lives under there is very important because men think their socks are hidden. The socks he chooses to wear come from the perception that he thinks no one else can see them. But what you find under there tells you what's going on behind the scenes in his life that he thinks is tucked away under the cover of his pants.

When you do ask him to lift his pant leg, prepare for one of these three reactions:

- *Reaction #1: Takes offense and makes excuses.* When you turn the spotlight on a man's socks, he might become suddenly defensive. Most likely he has something to hide, and he wasn't expecting you to call him out on it. If he tries to make you feel petty or superficial or tells you that they're *only* socks, don't let him. That's blaming, and he needs to start taking responsibility for his decisions—beginning with his socks.
- *Reaction #2: No reaction.* He couldn't care less. In which case, if you find that his socks rocket off the nasty chart, you may want to further your *sole* reconnaissance and find out what else he doesn't care about.
- *Reaction #3: Explanation.* He accepts responsibility for his choice in his nasty socks and gives an explanation as to why he's wearing them. Perhaps, they were his last clean pair. Perhaps, he went to the gym earlier and forgot to bring dress socks for his date. Or he can't throw them out because his late mother gave them to him for his birthday.

How a man pairs his shoes with socks is also a good indicator of how congruent he is with the different aspects of his life. Generally speaking there should be an easy upward "flow" from your man's shoes to his socks to his trousers. This flow means that most men will wear a pair of corresponding socks in color, texture, and thickness to blend with the color, texture, and thickness of his shoes. Ideally, it should barely be perceptible where one ends and the other begins. A man who has achieved such a balanced flow from his shoes to his socks to his trousers most likely has achieved the equivalent in his life.

The opposite can be said as well. One of the reasons why black shoes and white socks are considered a fashion faux pas is that they are disruptive. Opposite colors cut the flow from shoe to sock to trouser and are the equivalent of bad panty lines under a clingy skirt. If he hasn't achieved harmony between his socks and shoes, it's an indicator that he has difficulty balancing out other aspects of his life as well.

Achieving *shoe-to-sock harmony* can be difficult in the summer months when men wear shorts and they have to balance out a pair of hairy legs or chicken legs or both. Let's face it. Most men's legs look funny. Since men's legs aren't such art pieces as ours, it can be a challenge to incorporate them into the "outfit." This can be done by wearing ankle socks with sneakers so that the socks peek out just over the collar of the shoes but don't rise up the calf. Or they can opt for a simple summer sandal or flip flop that don't require any socks at all. Anything else can look really funny—especially dress shoes, shorts, and no socks.

In the summer months, it's best to judge a man's *sock-to-shoe* harmony based on his intent to achieve it rather than his actual ability to pull it off. And if you do find a man who can pull it off, go get him! He's a master.

Definition

Shoe-to-Sock Harmony—*The overall sense of balance a man achieves in his outward appearance by complementing his shoes with a flattering pair of socks.*

As you're asking your man to lift a pant leg, he may try to tell you that they're *just socks* and that he deserves a "Get Out of Bad Sock Jail Free" card, don't give it to him. This is why. How men do one thing is how they do all things. Socks complete the last leg of the outfit. Why go *almost* all the way only to stop? Men who couple even desirable shoes with unattractive socks generally aren't finishers. They might get close to the finish line, but they generally don't go the last ten yards.

Sole Profile: Put It All Together

You're ready for the sole profile shakedown. Simply use the information you've collected to answer these questions to learn more about how your man feels about himself, *really*.

Insert his name here ______________________________

1. What was your sole impression of his shoes?
2. What were your discoveries with your zoom lens?
3. What was the condition of his shoes?
4. What quick shoe connotations did you pick up on?
5. What did his shoes make him feel—younger, older, or just right?
6. What sole relativity moments did you have, if any?
7. What did you think of his sock-to-shoe harmony?
8. What surprises with his socks, if any, were "under there"?

Taking all your sole reconnaissance into account, do you think your man considers himself (circle one) a frog or a prince?

CHAPTER 7

Sole Reconnaissance

Sole Quote:

"Footwear tells the whole human story. It's all there from the animal hides that prehistoric cave dwellers wrapped around their feet to the high-tech boots worn by astronauts."

—Sonja Bata, owner of Bata Shoes

Rewind to Fast Forward

Sometimes the best way to predict the future is to take a sneaky peak into the past. History repeats. It may take two minutes or two thousand years, but just like a boomerang or bellbottoms, the past comes back to either hit you over the head or make your butt look big. In a relationship a man is supposed to sweep you off your feet, not knock you off your feet with his relationship history. If we don't want unwanted history to repeat in our romantic lives, we must start listening to what a man's shoes say today so that we don't repeat the same mistakes tomorrow. When a woman begins to make conscious choices about the quality of shoes she allows to walk into her life, that's when History becomes *Her*story.

Perhaps, you're left wondering, *Who is this* ____________ (fill in the superlative adjective) *guy I just met?* What if you haven't already worked together or been friends for ten years? What if you can't get the scoop from a mutual tell-it-all girlfriend? Perhaps you don't feel comfortable asking him that all-important, perennially awkward question, So, um, can you tell me about your past relationships?

If you're nervous that you don't have any background information on your new superman, don't worry. The truth is that you already do. Instead of running his plates, check out his shoes. They'll give you all the relationship history you can handle. Do you remember how everything we do, say, or think leaves a record or an imprint in the world around us? When you look at a man's shoes, you're seeing the sum total of every choice he's ever made in his life to decide to buy and wear those particular shoes.

When you're wondering if the milk has gone sour, you give it a sniff test before you drink it. Consider your answer to Pre-Relationship Question #3: What can you expect from him in the relationship? (the pre-relationship sniff test). Once you listen to what his shoes say about him, you'll know if he's any good. So sit back and relax because your man's shoes are about to take you on a virtual tour of his past relationship history.

A Nickel-Tour History of Men's Shoes

While we're in reverse, take a quick dip into the past. As men have evolved, so have their shoes, and the shoe industry has kept pace to tell us all about it.

Prehistoric Times: The pre-precursor to the modern UGG Boot was cavemen sewing animal skins into "foot bags" and wrapping them around their feet. At that point in pre-time, shoes reflected a primal attraction for warmth. Cavemen had no idea that ten thousand years later their foot bags would be fashionable and on back order for months at a time.

Ancient Roman Times:	Hip to the jive that the army that could walk the farthest won. The Romans conquered half the known world by hammering a few nails into the bottoms of their shoes. Today CEOs who are conquering the corporate world reconnect to their Roman roots by wearing Maximus-esque Man Sandals, although they skip the skirt and go for khaki short shorts instead.
Middle Ages:	Men discovered that stuffing their codpieces along with their long pointed shoes would attract not only a lady's attention but offend the church as well. This was the world's first and most glaring example of a man's Package Packaging Plan.
16th & 17th Centuries:	The original metrosexuals, "stylish" dandies and musketeers, wore high heels and boots adorned with large ruffles, pompoms, and soft satin bows. Their Fem Factor didn't stop at their toes but extended all the way up to their cascading curls. During these times, a woman definitely needed her own bathroom.

18th Century:	Men got off their high heels and onto their high horses with macho riding boots. The stiff boots made men feel like men again as it exaggerated their masculine swaggers. The trend eventually rode its way into Hollywood where the swagger hasn't stopped since. Only now men's riding boots are for motorcycles and are coupled with Top Gun flight glasses.
19th Century:	Life suddenly got a lot more comfortable as mass production made it affordable to produce shoes designed for the left *and* right foot.
20th Century:	As shoes became a matter of personal taste, the modern world was no longer ruled by function. Instead, the modern world was ruled by fashion, hype, and fads that Derek Zoolander exposed in Mugatu's global fashion conspiracy.
21st Century:	History completes its cycle as the modern UGG boot satisfies both our prehistoric need for warmth and our modern desire of self-expression. One cycle of history is completed and another begins as shoes transcend the necessary and become the answer to all women's relationship questions about the opposite sex.

Sole Reconnaissance: Closet Characteristics

People are not the only ones who experience a different quality of life depending on where they live. Shoes do too. Depending on the owner, the life experience (and expectancy) of a shoe varies from regularly polished and placed on a pedestal in a shoe cupboard to carelessly tossed on the floor and forced to comingle with his stinky laundry. Before entering a relationship with a man, you want to know exactly how his shoes live. Does he give his shoes enough space? Is he gentle with the suede? Does he support his shoes with *a* shoehorn? Does he *keep up with sole maintenance?*

All these aspects make up your man's three Closet Characteristics (Organization, Variety and Common Ground, and His Sole) and will give you a sneaky peek what to expect from him in the relationship. Knowing where and how your man's shoes live is like taking a snapshot of the future. How he treats his shoes is indicative of how he will treat all the other things in his life. Including you!

CLOSET CHARACTERISTIC #1: ORGANIZATION

You'll have to weasel your nose into his closet for this one, but now you know how to do it, and believe me it'll be worth it. How your man organizes his shoes is a good indication of how he organizes his life. Although you might be afraid to look, remember it's the truth that sets you free. Are his shoes tossed into a soupy mix that covers the closet floor? Or are they lined up exactly a quarter inch apart? Or are they stacked on top of each other? It's important that you become aware of your man's organizational trickles early on in the relationship. If you don't enjoy them now, most likely you won't be thrilled when his trickles turn into a hard rain. To get a weather report on what kind of trickles are coming your way, use Soleology's Relationship Organization Prediction Indicator to catch a glimpse of your future before it catches you.

Soleology's Relationship Organization Prediction Indicator

1. *Tangled mess:* Don't be surprised if your man spends half his life looking for something. Good thing you always know where his keys, wallet, and shoes are. You may want to do some additional Awareness Expansion to see if his tangled mess status doesn't bleed into other aspects of his life such as finances, relationships, or work.
2. *Loosely lined:* This is the type of man who rides the middle ground. He's loosely organized and moves forward at a relaxed pace that's right for him. He's flexible but knows the benefits of some focus and organization. He might not know where his shoes are, but he knows they're *somewhere* in the house.
3. *Systematic:* The sneakers are with the sneakers. The bowlers are with the bowlers. The two don't mix. This is a man who doesn't waste time. He knows what he wants, where to get it, and when to move on. He has a distinct awareness of himself and sticks to his schedule. Some people may think he's a stiff, but they count on him to get the job done. Yes, he knows exactly where his shoes, keys, and wallet are.
4. *Strict disciplined system:* Rigid and uncompromising, he may be prone to a meltdown if things don't go as he

planned or if *you* can't find his shoes. Since these guys think that they have a "no fail" system in place, don't be surprised if he blames you when he doesn't know where his shoes are.

Now, based on your sole reconnaissance, ask yourself, Can I share a closet with this man? If the idea makes you tear up, don't worry, there's hope. His and her closets can provide a lasting solution.

Soleological Bonus

How a man organizes his shoes also gives you a sign as to how reliable he is for a date. By looking at his shoes, you'll know what time you should actually be dressed and ready.

Tangled Mess

No rush. Also, you might want to call to remind him about the date 1/2 hour before the date.

Loosely Lined

He generally stays within a 1/2-hour radius of being on time.

Systematic

Eight o'clock is eight o'clock. Pick out your outfit the night before and be ready.

Strict Disciplined System

Don't be surprised if you hear his car pull up ten minutes early or if he wants to synchronize watches.

CLOSET CHARACTERISTIC #2: VARIETY AND COMMON GROUND

In art you need both positive and negative space to create a picture. Soleology is no different. That's why it's so important for you to be aware of who he isn't because that's a big part of who he is. In fact Jane Sheehan, famed UK foot reader, says "It's not just the shoes you wear that say a lot about you. It's also the shoes you buy and never wear." The variety in your man's footwear collection reveals the different roles he plays in life and the varied aspects of himself he chooses to express. Motorcycle boots among wingtips out him as a weekend road warrior. Or gold patent leather loafers among Bostonians can expose your middle manager by day is a "super freak" by night.

On the flip side, the common ground that your man's shoes share represents the side of him that he feels most comfortable with. For instance, a man who owns ten pairs of various athletic outdoor shoes is going to be of a different sort than a man who owns ten pairs of various Italian loafers. Once a man finds his niche in the world, he makes it known through his choice in shoes. Typically, one type of shoe, style, or brand will dominate his footwear arsenal.

If you start to see a change in the balance between the variety and common ground in his closet, it could be a sign that your man is either stepping up in life or letting more of his true self out. The positioning of his shoes can also give you a sign of what to expect in the relationship. Take careful notes on what new shoes are being introduced and how quickly they are brought in. Did they start at the back of his closet and slowly make their way to the front? Or did they instantly usurp the Alpha-Shoe position?

If your man's previous Payless wingtips have suddenly been replaced with John Lobb leather lovelies, it could mean a few things: (1) He just got a huge promotion. (2) He got an extreme shoe makeover. (3) Both. Either way, a change in the balance of power between variety and common ground—especially with a surprise upset in the Alpha-Shoe position—means big changes not only in his closet but also in his life.

Once you know the balance of variety and common ground in a man's shoes and their respective pole position, you can get an idea of what kind of a mood your man is in just by understanding where the shoes came from in the pecking order of his closet. For example, if your man is wearing his über fly, gold lamé, pimp-me-now shoes, he's probably not in the mood to talk about how things are going at work. That would disturb his Disco Moment. Yet, if he's wearing his Edward Green power presentation, corporate tassel tacklers—go for it. In fact, he would probably love it if you asked him all about his day at the office.

Sample Sole Profiling for Variety and Common Ground

Case Study #1

6 pairs of flip-flops in various states of wear

1 pair of dusty black wingtips tossed in the corner

Analysis: Open-toed free-flowing spirit. You won't find him at a board meeting unless it's at the beach. But don't count him out on being successful. He could own the beach you met him on and the gorgeous three-story house behind it. If this one lived in a van, most likely you wouldn't have found the wingtips—albeit dusty.

Case Study #2

6 pairs of brown leather slip-on moccasin-style tassel Italian loafers

1 pair Harley Davidson motorcycle boots, polished and new

Analysis: Yes! Sir meets I Think I Like It Here. You might not recognize the suited man you met Wednesday for lunch when he picks you up in his leather fringe outfit and motorcycle boots on Saturday. But at least you'll hear him coming on his Harley a mile away. And if his boots are still like new, it's a sign that this is just a weekend thing. Otherwise, unlike you, his boots wouldn't be looking so fine. In that case, you might need to consider how much time you actually want to spend on the back of his bike.

Case Study #3

6 pairs of various Birkenstock-style Earth shoes

1 pair flip-flops

Analysis: Earth walker who leaves only footprints. Quick! Hide your bootleg aerosol hair spray and don't mention your uncle's cattle ranch.

CLOSET CHARACTERISTIC #3: HIS SOLE

One of the best ways to discover what to expect from a man in a relationship is to discover his *sole's purpose.* What is it meant to do? Does it protect his feet? Perform? Conform? Does it integrate his foot into its natural surroundings or does it shelter him from it? Describe his sole to yourself. What is the thickness? Is it stiff? What is it made out of? Rubber? Leather? Is his sole smooth or jagged? Does it extend past his shoe? And what is the condition of his sole? Is it worn down? Is it thinning in bits? Or does it give him the support, care, and resilience a man needs to get where he wants to go?

Also, how does he treat his sole? Does he wear it down and then throw it away? Or does he keep his sole well maintained? Is he a fixer-upper, do-it-himself Shoe Goo kind of guy? Or does he leave the maintenance of his sole to a professional? What is his attitude toward sole maintenance? And how does he treat the person who takes care of his sole? Is he patient and understanding toward his sole when it starts to break down? Or does he become upset, short tempered, and sees it as a hassle? These are all important aspects to consider because whatever a man's sole needs, chances are he needs it too. And his attitude toward it is the same attitude he has toward the maintenance of his own self. Furthermore, you can expect that how a man treats his sole is how he treats himself and trickles down on how he will treat you in a relationship.

Definition

Sole's Purpose—*What a man's sole is meant to do on this earth.*

DR. SOLE

Q. *I'm dating one guy who only wears expensive designer shoes, but they are all run down and scuffed, and the soles are getting thin. Another guy I'm considering has terrible taste in shoes, but they are always impeccably clean and well maintained. Whom should I go for?*

A. The answer is simple. Go for the guy who you think will bring you the most happiness. It sounds like your designer man thinks that once he's got the "right" shoes, all his efforts can stop. He's forgotten about the maintenance side of life, especially when it comes to his sole. There's a high chance that he takes the same no-maintenance approach with his romantic relationships as well. Once he's done enough to snag you, all efforts stop. Yet, your other friend could be a diamond in the rough. Although you aren't attracted to his personal style, that can be worked on because what he's got going for him sounds like a solid sole to build on. Because your diamond in the rough takes excellent care of his shoes, most likely he'll take excellent care of you. Ask yourself, If I were a shoe, which man would I want to take care of my sole?

A Soleology Quickie

Short on time? Even if you don't have access to his closet, just one little question will score you loads of Soleological information. Ask your man, "If you were a shoe, what kind of shoe would you be?" Let him describe it to you and closely listen to what he says. Every detail counts. His answer tells you who he wants to be on a sole level. Then any sole reconnaissance you do later will tell you if his shoes match up or if they are miles away.

Put It All Together

What did your Sole Reconnaissance efforts come up with to answer Pre-Relationship Question #3: What can I expect from him in a relationship?

1. What quality of life are his shoes experiencing in his closet?
2. What type of an organizer is he? And how much time does that leave you to get ready before a date?
3. What variety of shoes does he have?
4. What do they have in common?
5. What shoe is in the Alpha-Shoe position?
6. What are the condition of his shoes and of their soles?
7. What do you think his sole's purpose is?

Based on what relationship trickles are coming your way, would you expect (circle one) spring showers, a tropical storm, or a hurricane in your relationship?

CHAPTER 8

Sex and His Sole

Sole Quote:

"Flowers in the desert don't pop their corks for just anyone."
—based on "Big Spender" (lyrics by Dorothy Fields)

Did you ever play the game when you go out for Chinese food with your friends and everyone reads their fortunes saying the same ending—in bed? Well, checking out a man's shoes can also let you know of your good fortune—in bed, which definitely puts a different spin on the fortune that reads, "You will be very satisfied soon." While reading this chapter, you might want to keep a bar of imported chocolate nearby. It's just a suggestion.

Being able to express your sexual self is an important part of a romantic relationship. Yet before we begin, there is one detail we should get out of the way: women are amazing, and men want to have sex with us. Now, that may sound like overstating the obvious, but often men get a bad rap for this. Just because a man wants to have sex with us doesn't mean we have to jump into bed with him—nor do we need to jump down his throat or get on his back about it. Instead, as you approach *sex* and the *sole*, feel free to bask in the fact that as a woman you are always desired. That gives you the freedom to choose a lover, not only because of his desire to have sex with you, but also because of what else he brings to the negotiating table.

When you're negotiating at the table, remember that

you're a flower in the desert—rare and precious. Flowers in the desert are admired, loved, and adored just for being themselves. Only the most worthy of admirers gets to take her home. And when it comes to adoration, you certainly don't want any slackers. Which is all the more reason to judge a man by his shoes. Your sole impression can spare you a night of *one-way romance.* Be gone that feeling of regret when you know that what you gave wasn't worth what you got. Just like eating a chocolate cupcake, Soleology wants you to wake up in the morning feeling satisfied that every calorie was worth it. So, the choice is yours. You decide what else a man has to offer besides the burning bulge growing in his pants. With Soleology, it's always ladies' choice. You decide if he gets to see and admire your flower in the desert.

Definition

One-Way Romance—*The inevitable disappointment of when there are two people in the bedroom, but only one is getting what he or she wants.*

Size Matters

Now, ladies, you knew this one was coming. We don't need Wonder Woman's lasso of truth to admit that when it comes to shoes, "the right fit" can take on a whole new meaning. Traditionally, the length of a man's foot has foreshadowed his ability to please us in bed. And it's true. What women have known for millennia has been scientifically proven only last year by a bunch of male scientists in Russia. Yes, it's official.

You can judge the size of a man's penis by the size of his feet. For our pleasure, our friendly shoe scientists have provided us with a formula to make an even more accurate prediction.

L = shoe size

H = penis size

H = (L + 5)/2

Now, you need to keep a condom *and* a calculator in your purse.

Shoe Size	**Penis Size**
7	______
8	______
9	______
10	______
11	______
12	______
13	______

So, what's next for our friendly scientists? Currently they are testing an equation to prove that the width of a man's foot determines the width of his penis. Again, we knew that.

WORKING IT

Whether it's padded bras or tummy slimmers, when it comes to attracting the opposite sex, women aren't the only ones working it.

Men are doing it too but keeping it on the down low. It's a Soleological Fact that 80 percent of men buy their shoes a half size too big. Which you may have to account for in the Shoe Size/Length chart you just cut out. Yet here's the kicker. In addition to men buying larger shoes, short men are wearing an "invisible" lift built into the sole of their shoes that secretly adds two to four inches to their height! And there's no way to find out until he's barefoot in the bedroom. Just like padded wonder bras, invisible shoes can lead to disappointment.

It's Hot in the Hot Tub

Whether a man is lusted after for his real or imagined length, he generally puts his best foot forward on a first date. Or, at least, what he thinks it is. That's why the shoes a man wears to pick you up, literally, tell you not only what he's attracted to but how he hopes to attract you as well. And since men are usually moving forward in the same direction—to the bed, you want to know what type of a night you're in for so you don't get stuck in a night of one-way romance or fumble football.

TEMPERATURE OF THE BEDROOM INDICATOR #1: PEAK PERFORMANCE

It doesn't matter if you're looking for a one-night wonder or a long-term relationship, before you trip and fall on a man's penis, pay special attention to how he puts *on* his shoes. This doesn't foreshadow length. It foreshadows *performance*. How he handles his shoes trickles down onto how he handles—or manhandles—you in bed. It's good to know what type of night you're in for—all knuckles, or not—because there's really nothing worse than that *after-attraction feeling* when you know that you got shortchanged in the romance department.

Definition

That After-Attraction Feeling—*The feeling of regret when you discover that what you thought you were attracted to wasn't worth the price you paid to satisfy your attraction.*

When you practice safe sole reconnaissance, you'll know what type of a night you're in for. Does he . . .

- Squish down the back of his shoe and shove his foot in?
- Fumble with his shoes and hop around?
- Put on his shoes while he's distracted by something else, like the TV?
- Use an apparatus for a smooth slide?
- Walk around with his shoes undone?
- Slide his foot in with care and finesse?

Sole Story

Latisha was visiting a friend in San Francisco when they decided to get all gussied up and head out for a big night in the city. It was about closing time in one of the lesser-known clubs in The Triangle. Latisha sat down at a table and began to yawn. Suddenly, a man pulled up a chair beside her. He introduced himself as Lawrence. Latisha instantly knew this was a ten-to-two Pickup. Lawrence tried various inroads with Latisha. He asked her if she went to school. How did she like San Francisco? Ultimately, Latisha wasn't interested.

When Lawrence noticed the bouncers starting to clear everyone out from the back, he gave it his last Hail Mary effort to have sex that night. Lawrence stared straight into her eyes, put his hand on Latisha's knee, and told her with a definite persuasion, "You know," he said, "I go down." In that moment Latisha had three thoughts: The first was, You all do. The second was, Well, maybe. It had been a while. Then the lights flicked on and she looked down at his shoes. His laces were a knotted mess and his shoes were as disheveled as he was. Latisha removed Lawrence's hand from her knee and spoke her third thought out loud, "No thanks," she said, "Good night."

Definition

The Ten-to-Two Pickup—*After striking out all night, a man gives his hope of sex a last minute, last-ditch effort in the wee moments before a bar closes.*

TEMPERATURE OF THE BEDROOM INDICATOR #2: ROCK MY SOCKS

In addition to how a man slides on his shoes, men's socks are also an indicator of his libido and prowess to please. Whether men realize it or not, their socks are the equivalent of women's lingerie. If you decide "to go horizontal" with an incredibly lucky man—or if you're already doing the horizontal mambo—don't forget to ask him to lift a pant leg. It's the equivalent to his going for a panty peek when you walk up the stairs. What you find under there will give you an indication of what type of night he's in the mood for. Then you can work your angle from there.

Men's Socks	***Women's Lingerie Equivalent***
Ratty balled yellow tube socks	Period panties
Slipper socks	Cozy bathrobe
Thermals	Flannel PJs
Athletic mid-calf tube socks	Athletic sports bra
Athletic knee-highs	Granny pants
Athletic ankle socks	Sexy boy-cut hot pants
Cotton socks	Matching cotton bra and panty set

Argyle	Fashion-print thigh highs
Nylon sheer-ribbed trouser socks	Fishnets and a peek-a-boo nightie
Sock garters	Garters
Barefoot	Commando

If you're wearing fishnets and his socks are the equivalent of period panties, he's probably not on the same sexual wavelength. Which can make any attraction for him head south very quickly. The unfortunate coupling of fabulous shoes and disastrous socks is yet another example of how a man can go so right and then so very wrong. Unforgivable socks can completely cancel out good behavior on a date because any level of attraction you have had going for him is suddenly flushed down the toilet. He may have opened your door and held your hand. He may even have thrown his coat over a puddle so that you wouldn't dirty your shoes. But when he sat down, his pant leg lifted and exposed his horrid balled yellow athletic tube socks poking out of his black dress shoes. No matter how much a man tries to compensate for his disastrous socks, once the soufflé falls nothing can save it.

TEMPERATURE OF THE BEDROOM INDICATOR #3: THE SCOTTISH KILTIE TICKLERS

The French aren't the only ones who have cornered the market on various ticklish items. The Scottish have their version as well. Do you know what Scottish men wear under their traditional kiltie skirts? Nothing. That is why when a man is ready for some hanky panky, he doesn't wear anything under his *Scottish kiltie tickler* loafers either. Instead, he flashes his naked ankles and lets your mind wander as to what else he might—or might not—be wearing. Don't be surprised if you get a lunchtime bootie call when your middle-management man is wearing his Scottish kiltie ticklers without socks. Just make sure that if you two have fun in the copy room, there isn't any photographic evidence left behind.

For a double kinky twist, some sex maniacs combine the tickle my tassel with the Scottish kiltie tickler. In such cases, be prepared for some major footsie. When you experience what these tickle masters can do for you under the table, you might just ask him to leave his loafers on in bed. Tack on an extended textured tip, and you're halfway to heaven. And if he's wearing such playful little things on his feet, imagine what he's tucked away in the closet at home.

Definition

Scottish Kiltie Ticklers—*You know that delightful little thing that looks like a ruffle and sticks out just below the top of his loafers? Well, you might want to give it a whirl.*

THE UNFORGIVABLES

While taking the temperature of the bedroom, there are some things that can leave it rather cold:

Black Shoes, White Socks. Why do men do it? Perhaps it's a government agency secret—or an X-File. Michael Jackson does it. But does your date really want to be associated with a man who has a theme park in his backyard?

Socks and Sandals. A most unfortunate coupling to be

sure. Socks and sandals are a perennial fashion footwear faux pas, but it may be worth your while to do some sole reconnaissance and investigate why he's breaking one of the steadfast rules of attraction. Is he German? Socks and sandals are practically Germany's national costume. Next, check the temperature of the room. Perhaps his feet are dangerously cold, and he's left without a suitable alternative? And third, do *you* wear socks and sandals? If your answer is yes, he could well be your solemate—in bed.

Do you want to have fun? Do you want to have a good time? Ask him to wear these shoes!

The Ben Sherman: The Double

Kenneth Cole Reaction: The Big Thrill

Unlisted: Groove Tube

Steve Madden: WOW

Salomon: Power Slide

Sorel: Jackhammer

Dunham: Cloud Nine

Lacoste: Rotate Plus and Turbo Curve

Knowing His Fem Factor: Don't Hate Me Because I'm More Beautiful

When it comes to expressing our sexual selves, men and women have both a feminine side and a masculine side. There's Yin in the Yang. And Yang in the Yin. One cannot exist without the other. It is like trying to make chicken soup without the soup or the chicken. Impossible. In every relationship there is a push and a pull, a give and a take, a feminine and a masculine energy.

It's the same with men's shoes. Some are more Yang. Some are more Yin. It's good to know which way your man swings with his Fem Factor because a relationship works best when both parts complete the whole—not compete for the same part. Determining the Fem Factor of a man's shoes will give you an insight into whether you need to hide your styling products and whether you can co-exist peacefully together while sharing a single bathroom sink.

The more Yin you find in your man's shoes could mean that you are coupling with a Yin Man. A Yin Man is someone who not only enjoys all the benefits of being a man but also wants to be treated like a lady. For example, this is a man who wants to lead the relationship *and* wants you to cater to his feelings. In which case, you may want to tell him that feminine is *not* the new masculine. Relationships with Yin Men can be very tricky. Especially if you are both vying for the position of Alpha Yin. Or if you share a bathroom and have only a half an hour to get ready. Yet, relationships teach us to share. If you're dating a Yin Man and you're willing to share your Alpha-Yin status, here are a few tips that can make life, and getting ready, easier. Especially when you're all done up, don't let him steal your thunder. Make sure he still opens the door for you so that you can make an entrance. Not him.

WHAT TO DO IF YOU'RE LIVING WITH A YIN MAN

Make sure you have the following:

- 2 full-length mirrors
- 2 medicine cabinets
- 2 hairdryers
- His and her bathrooms
- His and her closets
- Separate styling products
- Separate stylists
- Separate salons
- Separate credit card accounts

Yin Men can be as easy to spot as dandruff on black cashmere or as difficult to identify as a really good "practically" Prada purse. Yet there are some definite tip-offs. First of all, most Yin Men love their ankles. While it's true that they usually have lovely ankles, make sure that his admiration for his own ankles doesn't detract from his admiration for yours. Second, Yin Men shave more than just their face, which in some cases is actually quite a good idea. The third tip-off is that they keep and maintain their skin just as soft and dewy as yours. Yet, the biggest tip-off of all is that just like women adore a strappy sandal—so do they. These days Yin Men have their own version of the strappy sandal. They usually are a flat (sans heel), open-toe leather slip-on summer sandal. The straps may cup his big toe or gracefully interweave over the top of his foot.

The point is to make his feet look pretty, especially if he has just had a pedicure. You'll often find a soft breeze of white linen trousers brushing gently over the top. Yet another Yin man tip-off.

The Soleology Fem Factor Yin/Yang Continuum

Where do your man's shoes land on the Soleology Fem Factor Yin/Yang Continuum? This is important so you know what to expect from him not only in the bedroom but also in the bathroom and how to divvy up your future closet space.

The Fem Factor Yin/Yang Continuum The Elements of Yin and Yang

YIN		YANG
Thin . . . Light . . . Open . . . Soft	⟵⟶	*Thick . . . Heavy . . . Closed . . . Hard*
All Yin	A Sprinkling of Each	All Yang

Sole Story

That morning, it wasn't only the coffee that was hot. Vienna was enjoying her morning Starbucks caffeine fix just as much as she was enjoying admiring the man sitting opposite her on one of those sage cushy couch seats. Seated next to him was a friend who was equally tall, dark, and handsome.

Yet Vienna noticed that the object of her affection was also in admiration of something else. And it wasn't another woman. Vienna saw him lovingly gaze down on his soft suede strappy summer sandals no fewer than eight times. She had to admit they were lovely, but just not the type of shoe she actually wanted to see on a guy. Hiding behind her steaming coffee, Vienna also noticed that he was checking out his friend's shoes as well. When she overheard one of them say, "Thanks, I just got them," she felt like these guys were stealing her line.

Vienna was confused. She didn't get the gay vibe from either one of them, but as handsome as her Adonis was, she preferred her men a little less self-shoe absorbed. And she certainly didn't want to experience shoe envy in her relationship.

Vienna finished her coffee and headed for the door. She took one last glance at her Adonis. His eyes were still glued to his feet as she watched him wiggle his toes in admiration. As Vienna took her coffee to go, she changed the name of her ex-future husband from Adonis to Narcissus

A Soleology Quickie: Superhero Fruit Boots

While discussing a man's Fem Factor, there's really no way to approach this subject lightly. If superheroes are supposed to be a male sex symbol and make women swoon, why do they wear high leather boots, bright tights, and matchy-matchy outfits?

Since every superhero only becomes really "super" when he puts on his matchy-matchy tight leather boot outfit, does that mean his power really comes from his femininity? Think about it—you never saw the Marlborough Man wearing bright green tights, a cape, or a cup.

Superhero Fruit Boot Checklist

Batman ✓

Superman ✓

Flash ✓

Captain America ✓

Spiderman ✓

Mr. Incredible ✓

Sole Story

The first date Lizzie had with her latest and greatest whom she met in a Hollywood bar was a picnic in the park. It was a gorgeous day, blue skies, and hot. She arrived to a lovely picnic spread all ready for her over a blue gingham blanket. Everything looked perfect. As Lizzie kicked off her shoes and relaxed, she noticed that he didn't. In fact, he was wearing thick black leather lace-up oxfords on a 90-degree Sunday afternoon. She invited him to take his shoes off and put his feet in the grass. "No way," he said, "my feet are disgusting. I haven't had a pedicure in over a week." Lizzie looked down at her own pedicure which was well over two weeks old. Since Lizzie preferred being the woman in the relationship, she decided she should let that fish go.

Girls Gone Wild: The Men's Shoe Edition

Let's get right to the point: it takes two to tango. If you're single and you want to play the relationship game—you need to meet someone to partner with. The good news is that men are all around us. Everywhere you look, there they are—at work, the grocery store, on the beach, in museums. That is why selecting a man is a ladies' choice. For a moment, imagine yourself in the shoe section of your favorite department store. You pick up each shoe, turn it around, and look for any bad spots before you buy them. Judging a man by his shoes takes the same approach. His shoes will tell you if there are any "bad spots" before you take him home. Just like you shop for what

Better-Than-Sex Shoes

Ten Reasons Why Shoes Are Better Than Men

1. They come in pairs.
2. We pick their size.
3. They prefer to be fixed.
4. They always know how to complement us.
5. They wait for us right where we left them.
6. If we keep the receipt, they're returnable.
7. They don't mind being cleaned up.
8. They like it when we "step on them."
9. They always know how to make us feel better.
10. They don't get jealous if we've had multiple shoe experiences.

you want to wear, eat, or drive, you can shop for a man. Which makes playing the relationship game a lot more fun.

The best way to go man shopping is to host a Girls Gone Wild Night Out: Men's Shoes Edition. It's just as entertaining as one of those "intimate accessories" panty parties, but this event gives you the chance to meet actual men—not just their rubber vibrating counterparts. If you're feeling bold, host your first Girls Gone Wild Night Out at your local meet and greet. Perhaps it's at a bar or your favorite music venue. Get there early before the deluge of men appear so that you can go over your mission with your girlfriends. It could be simply to practice your Soleology skills and hone your sole impressions. Or you can shave your legs, gussy up, and arrive with the actual intent to meet men.

If you and your cohorts are feeling like you want a little practice first, you can also host a Girls Gone Wild Night right in the privacy of someone's home. Everyone can share their sole stories over a few bottles of wine. Or if there's a man you're considering, bring in a pair of his shoes for a group evaluation. The latter of which will take some stealth maneuvers to obtain the sample. Whatever you decide, when it comes to planning your Girls Gone Wild Night, the rules are—there are no rules. Do it your way.

If you do decide to get your crew together to dish it up and meet and greet for a Girls Gone Wild Night Out, here are a few tips. First, let a man know that you're looking at his shoes. It's a great way to start a conversation. You don't even have to mention this book. Say you're helping a friend do a Soleology experiment. You are. Only that friend is you. And if a guy asks, "What's Soleology?" Give him a wink and flash your most beautiful smile. Tell him, Soleology is a great way to meet men. Then leave it right there. If the fish on your line has two brain cells to rub together, he'll pick up right where you left off.

On a Girls Gone Wild Night Out, there's no reason to feel shy or silly when you ask a man about his shoes—especially if you are at a bar. A man will appreciate the fact that after staring at you all night, you made it easy for him to strike up a conversation. The fact that you struck up the conversation isn't important. What's important is that you let him carry it. Besides, as long as a man is talking to you, he thinks that he's getting closer to sex while you're gleaning important information about him from his shoes.

The only possible buzz kill at the end of a Girls Gone Wild Night Out are *Sole goggles*. Just like beer goggles can land you a less-than-charming Prince Charming, sole goggles can be blamed for a man showing up at your door in blown-out hemp-huraches—or worse. If you see a girlfriend sporting a thick pair of sole goggles, cut her off from the bar and give her a *reality sole check.*

Definitions

***Sole* Goggles**—*A visual impairment of judging a man by his shoes, usually due to an excess of alcohol.*

Reality Sole Check—*An emergency intervention between your visually impaired friend and a very bad pair of shoes.*

Top 5 Reasons to Organize a Girl's Gone Wild Night Out

1. It's a great way to meet as many men as you can handle and check out their shoes.
2. It's a great way to sharpen your flirting skills.
3. It's a great way to meet as many men as you can handle and check out their shoes.
4. It's a great way to hone your man-hunting instincts.
5. It's a great way to meet as many men as you can handle and check out their shoes.

DR. SOLE

Q. *I'm way too shy to approach a man even if I'm just talking to him about his shoes. Is there anything else I can do?*

A. If you're not feeling up to openly sole profiling a man, it's okay. While out with your girlfriends, try this instead:

imagine the shoes a man wears are like his own little personal ad in the newspaper or on Match.com. What do they say? How do they describe their owner? □

Sample Personals Ads

The Shoes: Smooth leather slip-on loafers with elastic side-band entry.
The Ad: "Well polished, tailored, and smooth, I like to slip in and out of situations. I don't waste my time with anything as time consuming as laces. I'm rigid, yet there's some room for flexibility as long as it's a quick, smooth fit."

The Shoes: Retro skate shoes with wide white laces and a Velcro secure top.
The Ad: "Hey, you're kinda cute. Me too. I'm young and fun. A kid at heart. I may be forty years old and own my own hedge fund, but you'll still see me shredding at the Skate Park. Later skater."

Putting It All Together

How hot is hot? Based on your sole reconassiance, what is the answer to Pre-Relationship Question #4: What can you expect from him in the relationship—in bed? Try answering the following questions to know what you should wear or should *not* be wearing on your next date:

1. Based on his shoe size/length conversion chart would you consider him for the horizontal mambo?

2. Do you find yourself getting a little hot around the neck when you watch him put on his shoes?
3. Do his socks complement your lingerie?
4. Depending upon his Fem Factor, do you need to share your Alpha Yin status?
5. Say your man's shoes wrote his personals ad, how would it read?

Based on my answers I (circle one) would or would not pop my cork.

PART THREE

Soleology: How to Work It

What if you could *go from* letting relationships happen to you to making the right relationships happen? And what if instead of going after a man, you could make him come to you? Well, you can.

Once you know the reasons behind why a man wears the shoes he does, it puts you in the driver's seat in the relationship. You can anticipate his next move. More importantly, you decide if you want to be around when he makes it. Traditionally, a woman's focus has been on making herself attractive to "catch" a man. Yet once you know what makes a man tick, you can move from dropping your line in the water to being *the catch*.

Once you understand how attraction works, you can use it to expand your man options and draw to you only what you want and leave the riffraff behind. The truth is that there are more than a few Shoe Sharks in the water. Soleology shines a light on whether a man uses his shoes as bait to hook you because he wants to make you happy or simply to satisfy his own desire.

CHAPTER 9

Sole Attraction

Sole Note:

If your man wasn't attracted to his shoes, they wouldn't be on his feet!

Once you start listening to what men's shoes say about them, you'll notice that their shoes spill the same beans over and over. A man's shoes tell you exactly what he is attracted to in his life. If he's wearing business-class no-loafing loafers, then he is attracted to success. If he wears forever-young skater-dude sneakers with checkerboard laces, then he is attracted to finding the fountain of youth. If your man is sporting a leather and stud roughrider manly Marlborough man combo, he is attracted to protecting his "tough guy" image. And it's your sole impression that will tell you whether underneath his tough guy image your man is a real bear or teddy bear.

Whether your man wears a particular pair of shoes every day or it sits in the closet collecting dust, each pair he owns reveals his past, present, and future attractions. I'm not talking about the kinds of attractions that define him as a boob or a butt man, but the kinds of attractions that define a man as a person—which can make or break a relationship with you. The question *is*, Are you mutually attracted to experiencing the same future as he is through his choice of shoes?

Past Attractions

A popular saying is, "We are what we can't get rid of." The shoes a man keeps for prosperity or old times' sake tell you what he hopes one day to experience once again to relive the memory. When you conduct sole reconnaissance, pay extra attention to his shoes that are collecting dust. Are they beachy? Are they something he would wear on vacation? Are they adventurous? Perhaps what he wore when he climbed Mt. Kilimanjaro?

Now, you can use this information to appear absolutely magical in his eyes. Devise a special surprise for him when he can dust off those shoes and breathe new life into them. You don't have to book a flight to Africa but suggest a date where he could dust off his hiking shoes and put them on his feet again. Or the next time you cook him dinner, choose a theme that invites him to pull out his *memory lane shoes* from the back of his closet. That is certainly one way to get on his good foot. He'll be mesmerized and left wondering how you "just knew" everything about him.

Definition

Memory Lane Shoes—*The shoes in a man's closet that have no particular function other than to remind him of the fun and exciting guy he used to be.*

Present Attractions

A man's present attractions are represented by his Everyday Shoes. These are the shoes your man will wear as often as he can, even if they don't quite fit the circumstances. Although most men spend the majority of their week at work, Everyday Shoes are the ones that your man wears the most when he gets to choose what he puts on his feet.

A man who wears his "dress up" flip-flops to a fancy dinner is someone who is attracted to an open-and-free feeling wherever he goes. Watch him squirm in anything else—especially in a pair of shiny tuxedo rentals. While a man who wears wingtips or their equivalent to the beach is someone who is attracted to maintaining status and authority even when everyone else is "hanging loose." It's important that you feel comfortable spending every day with your man's Everyday Shoes because the four of you will be hanging out a lot!

Future Attractions

While conducting *sole* reconnaissance, sometimes you'll find shoes in your man's closet that he hasn't worn yet. They are in-the-box new, and perhaps he even put them in the Alpha-Shoe position.

Pay special attention to these shoes because they are the shoes that he hopes to wear someday. Perhaps, he's saving up toward a safari in the jungle, which would explain the sudden pair of all-terrain hikers. Or he's a recent college grad who just bought his first pair of "profession" shoes. Either way, these dream shoes are like the "skinny dresses" women buy in the hopes that they can fit into them someday.

While considering entering into a relationship with him, think what direction these shoes point to. If the two of you met backpacking in Hawaii and suddenly he's got a growing collection of croc-moc loafers, you can expect a change in the wind. Also, if you are already in a relationship with a man and you discover a pair of Ahoy Matie! white rubber deck sailing shoes, take the hint and be the first to suggest a sailing trip. Perhaps, even take a trip to the boat broker. You just might win a permanent position on his crew as best mate.

This Thing Called Attraction

So, what is it that makes us buy one shoe over another? It's called attraction and unless you've got a handle on attraction, it's got a handle on you. Attraction is a tricky, slippery thing. Since both sexes are controlled by attraction, it's good to know what kind of animal you're dealing with. Attraction is a force that is stronger than gravity. Gravity keeps our feet on the ground. Attraction sends us into orbit at warp speed. Attraction makes us do some pretty crazy things like stalk a guy or call him a hundred times just to hear the sound of his voice. Just like women, men are victims of attraction too. That's why they do unmanly things for us like write us poems, serenade, massage our feet, send us flowers, or give piggyback rides. It also makes a man do things like buy a pair of Harley Davidson motorcycle boots, although he doesn't own a motorcycle.

Attraction makes us think beyond the rational and enter the world of compulsion. Its influence trickles down into all our decisions and makes us obsess over the object of our desire until we commit whatever is necessary to have it. Trying to function under the Attraction Mind Melt can feel like riding a bucking bronco or being sucked into a black hole. It can feel like a wild roller coaster ride that doesn't end. When you start feeling out of control, consider yourself under the control of the Attraction Mind Melt.

Women know firsthand the effect attraction has on us. It happens the minute we walk into our favorite shoe store. There they are—hundreds of shoes on display solely for our pleasure. Instantly, you dismiss some shoes. You give others a second look but nonetheless move on. Then there are some shoes that you have to have. Suddenly you're considering a second mortgage. You would rather spend your last penny at the register than leave the store without your leather lovelies. They may not fit. They may defy gravity and reason. The price may be more than your monthly grocery bill, but you *have to have them.*

The same thing happens the moment you walk into a bar. You're feeling great and looking fab. Perhaps you're wearing the same hot shoes you just bought. You scan the scene. There are hundreds of men, and you're rubbing elbows with them. Instantly, you dismiss some men. Nope. Never. Not on his life. Other guys get a second look but nonetheless are dropped into the *circular file.* Then there are a few men who you feel like you *have to have.* They may have obscene tattoos, tight jeans, or smell, but they exude a certain "je ne sais quois" which overrides any red-flag objections your sensibility has to giving them your number. Under these conditions, consider your brain officially under the power of the Attraction Mind Melt.

Definitions

The Circular File—*Where men are sent after they have been disqualified from playing the relationship game with you.*

The Attraction Mind Melt—*The most powerful energetic force in this dimension that melts our brains until we commit whatever is necessary to possess what we are attracted to.*

Whether it's shoes or men, your mind is being warped under a force more potent than anything known to our species. This force is so powerful that it turns even the most intelligent human brains into instant wanton mush. The Attraction Mind Melt makes us feel like we *have to have* anything. What's worse is that it convinces us to do anything to get it. That is regularly reflected in our credit card statements and/or level of regret.

The *power of attraction* is so compelling that it can override even the most resolute conviction. You may find yourself doing things you know aren't good for you like dating a bad boy. It isn't logic or logical, yet the power of attraction dominates your sensibilities and makes you desire to possess the object of your attraction, no matter what the cost.

Five signs that your mind is being warped by the Attraction Mind Melt:

1. One-track mind.
2. High levels of salivation.
3. Dangerous levels of irritability or grouchiness until you satisfy said attraction.
4. Inability to satisfy your attraction. You only want more.
5. Friends refuse to call because that's all you ever talk about.

Attraction, Distraction, and Answers

When we enter a relationship with a man while under the Attraction Mind Melt, it's understandable why we become so upset when it tanks. The Attraction Mind Melt makes us think that all the wonderful feelings of connection and love we experience in the relationship only comes from being with that particular man. Which is an interesting notion, yet simply not true.

After a relationship spontaneously combusts—instead of saying "Next!"—women under the Attraction Mind Melt get down on themselves and scour their brains for an explanation of what they did "wrong" when in fact they did everything right. While in this state, women are vulnerable to the *attraction quick fix*. This is because the Attraction Mind Melt makes us think that what makes us happy lives outside ourselves. It convinces us that we must find something or someone else to make us feel better. Just like the hair of the dog, the attraction quick fix—whether a rebound man or retail therapy—substitutes one attraction for another. That's why it is only temporarily effective. If you find yourself *attraction jumping* between a new man and new shoes, consider yourself stuck in the *attraction loop*. Since any quick fix is only that—quick—it keeps you coming back for more because you never feel satisfied.

Definitions

Attraction Jumping—*The instant gratification of substituting one attraction for another.*

Attraction Loop—*The juggling of attractions from one to the other to escape temporarily the inevitable Attraction Detox.*

Attraction Quick Fix—*Whatever makes women feel better instantly but only for an instant after a relationship spontaneously combusts.*

DR. SOLE

Q. *Whenever I see a man in a pair of sensitive-man soft suede sandals, I can't say no. What do I do?*

A. The next time you feel that you have to have him, try the Soleology Walk-Away Test to see if he is something you really need or even want in your life. When a pair of sensitive-man sandals starts talking to you, before you book your wedding in Vegas, walk away—if only to the bathroom. Once you remove yourself from the temptation, observe your thoughts. Do you continue to obsess over his shoes? Are they still talking to you? And if they are, what are they saying? Or have you moved on, and if asked about your sensitive man, you would answer, "Who?" Walking away pulls you out of the Attraction Mind Melt and lands you back into the rational. By observing your *attraction reactions*, you'll know if his are a pair of shoes worth pursuing. ☐

Definitions

Attraction Reactions—*The sudden impulses we experience that make us feel a certain way without consciously thinking about it first.*

The more you attraction jump, the longer you put off the inevitable unavoidable *Attraction Detox*. Admittedly, there's no fun way to pull off a Band Aid. Nor is there is a fun way to go through the attraction detox. Whatever you do, it's going to hurt because you're dealing with a sensitive wound. Whether dealing with Band-Aids or the Attraction Detox, there are several ways you can go about it:

1. Rip it off in one swift stroke.
2. Tug slowly at it bit by bit.
3. Get drunk, attraction jump, and forget about it temporarily. That is, until it starts hurting again.

If you opt for #3, prepare to go deeper into Attraction Detox debt—which you must pay off eventually.

Stop here. Take a deep breath. The good news is that you don't ever have to be controlled by your attractions again. Soleology offers an Attraction Rx. Once you understand what a man is attracted to and why you are attracted to him, then attraction doesn't have a thing on you. If life were a deck of cards—attraction is the joker. The joke is that you have to go out and get what you want. Instead, when you learn to leverage attraction, you can learn to bring whatever you want to you.

Definitions

Attraction Detox—*The process of liberating yourself from your attractions to a particular man or shoe that may be momentarily painful but satisfying in the long run.*

Soleology's Attraction Rx—*Your light saber in the dark.*

Soleology's Attraction Rx, Part 1

GUARANTEES RESULTS IN THREE EASY STEPS!

1. Write all the qualities you are attracted to in your boyfriend/husband/lover/date or object of your desire.
2. Develop the same qualities within yourself.
3. Watch what happens. Poof! Just like magic, the attraction goes away.

Congratulations! You are no longer controlled by the Attraction Mind Melt.

If you are attracted to a man's sense of adventure—pack your bags and go on a trip! If you are attracted to a man's sense of accomplishment, start doing what you've always dreamed of accomplishing yourself. If you are attracted to your man's artistic qualities, start painting. The magic is that once you have what you want, you get more of it.

Using Soleology's Attraction Rx will change your pole

position in the relationship game from wanting the solemate of your dreams to having the solemate of your dreams. At first, it may sound counterintuitive, but this is how this whole thing works. We must first become the very thing we desire before we can attract it. Then it seems—as if by magic—all that we ever dreamed of in a solemate suddenly appears behind us in line at the grocery store. Just like in the Impulse commercial—when a man you've never met before suddenly buys you flowers, you've become a Master of Attraction.

Once you begin to leverage attraction into your romantic life, you'll no longer have to search for what you desire. Flowers don't chase after the bees. So be gone the days when you have to chase a man. He'll come to you. Instead of looking for what you want, you're free to spend your time and energy in more creative pursuits, like enjoying what you have. Which will allow your life to open up in ways you never imagined and bring you even more happiness. Remember, once you stop looking for what you want, you will have more time to enjoy it.

Definition

Master of Attraction—*Anyone who uses the knowledge that when you already are whatever it is that you desire, it comes to you.*

CHAPTER 10

Shoe Sharks

SoleQuote:

"A well-heeled man is heavenly. If he doesn't half-ass it with his shoes, he won't half-ass it with you."

—Ali Gentz, Los Angeles fashion buyer

Remember how all men want to have sex with us? Well, don't put it past them to try to stir up some Attraction Mind Melt magic of their own. When it comes to packaging their package, men certainly aren't above a little marketing. Consider what shoes men wear like their own little marketing kits. While there's truth in advertising, Soleology exposes a man's *Package Packaging Plan* for what it is—a thinly disguised advertising campaign to have sex with you. While some men invest in well-heeled shoes, others try to skate by hoping you won't notice their less than best-foot-forward indiscretions. Yet, what men don't realize is that women do notice—*everything*. When it comes to sealing the deal, you want to make sure that the merchandise that comes inside the box isn't disappointing.

Admittedly, some Package Packaging Plans manipulate your attractions to try to suck you into a long-lasting loving relationship. This is a man who wants you to know that your package and his package will be very happily packaged together. In fact Allan Flusser, a world-renowned men's clothing designer, describes men's shoes as "foot decorum" as he muses that "any man who respects quality footwear is likely to achieve success because he understands the value of working from the bottom up." Now, he didn't specify if he meant success in work or romantic relationships. Yet, *we can assume* that he inferred both.

As much as some men may want a loving relationship, there are some Shoe Sharks swimming in the water that you should know about. They, too, are Masters of Attraction and use their shoes to lure you in. That is another reason why your sole impression is more useful than a can of mace in your purse. When you use it, you'll instantly know who is a shark in sheep's shoes. And you won't ever have to be bitten by a Shoe Shark again.

Definitions

Shoe Shark—*A man who uses his shoes to attract women for less-than-honorable reasons.*

Package Packaging Plan—*The shoes men wear with the inner intent to woo women.*

While face-to-face with a Shoe Shark, it's important to know that not all Package Packaging Plans are designed with your best interest at heart. Instead, your interest lies somewhere near the heart of a Shoe Shark's bottom. And when it comes to packages, he's only concerned with servicing his own.

Soleology documents the three most common Shoe-Shark Package Packaging Plans. They are known as the No Approach, the Bait and Switch, and the Take Back. Each of these comes highly *not* recommended. Once you see them for what they are, no longer will you be wooed by their sales sizzle. Nor will you be left to read between the lines. Because when you judge a man by his shoes, you'll know who he is without having to read the fine print. And what his shoes say about him will become as easy to read as a highway billboard.

Shoe-Shark Package Packaging Plan #1: The No Approach

THE SHOES

Unforgivable, no effort shoes. Old. Tired. Scuffed. Falling apart. Blown out. Floppy soles. Possibly borrowed or "rescued" from a roommate's trash can.

THE SELL

The No-Approach Shoe Shark will wear some scabby shoes and then try to woo you with his "relaxed" attitude coupled with a "you're lucky to have me" air. Yet he has actually stolen your line. You are a flower in the desert. Men are meant to hold and keep your attention—not the other way around.

The No-Approach Shoe Shark will try to convince you that anything more than what little he has to offer is either elitist or part of a commercial conglomerate conspiracy. He will also try to convince you that what little he has "all *could* be yours." It's an interesting concept, yet take a look around. Do you really want to sit on a couch he scored from a back alley? Also, remember that the word "could" is a conditional modal verb. Exactly what condition is separating you from all that he has to offer? And do you even want what "could be" conditionally yours?

Don't say yes, if your Sole Impression says no. And be careful that he doesn't try to make you feel like a snob for calling him out on his scabby shoes. If his shoes are not so nice, then neither is he—especially if he tries to make you feel bad for walking away. Typically, these are the guys who go for insecure women. Instead of treating them like queens, he tries to make them think he's a king.

Sole Story

Marianne's date, Leo, showed up at her door in a pair of threadbare, blown-out canvas sneakers. His big toe had burst a hole through the faded red fabric and the rubber sole flopped around and squeaked as he walked Marianne to his car. Marianne knew she should have immediately excused herself with a sudden case of emphysema or allergies. Anything. But her mother taught her to see the good in people; so despite what her sole impression told her about Leo's shoes, Marianne felt obligated to continue with the date.

Marianne knew they were going to see a movie, but what she didn't expect was that the theater was his beach pad. As Leo opened the door to his crumbling "rustic" abode, Marianne detected the unmistakable stench of spilled beer. The carpet smelled like an old dog, the main decoration was a lava lamp, and the walls were painted sensuous burgundy. Leo gestured majestically to what he referred to as the couch of love. Marianne hesitated to sit down. And when she did, the couch felt damp. That was it. Everything from his shoes to his apartment was broken, smelled, and grossed her out. Marianne tried to excuse herself politely by saying she suddenly remembered that she had to make an urgent phone call. "What's you're problem?" Leo said. "Too stuck up for the beach?"

As Marianne bolted for the door, she heard Leo say under his breath, "Fucking princess. Doesn't know what she's missing." Luckily for Marianne, her mom taught her not only to see the good in people but also to always bring enough cash on a date for a taxi home.

RED FLAG SHOES

Sometimes even in your dreams a banana is just a banana. And in Soleology, a red flag is a red flag. Here is a small sampling of red flags that you may find waving over men's shoes.

Jellies: Sure, The Dude wore them in the *Big Lebowski*, but honesty would you really want to date *The Dude*?

Espadrilles: If a man is going for the romantic Venetian look, he might be best served actually to be in Venice, Italy.

Overhang: Generally, women enjoy it when men hang low, but it's a no-go with their shoes. He's dragging. If he can't support his own feet, can he support you?

Blown Out: Just because they make the same floppy sound, it doesn't qualify them as a pair of flip-flops. And just like you can't drive a car with a blown-out tire, a man with blown-out shoes is going nowhere fast.

Cracked Sole: Anything built on a cracked foundation eventually will fall. Be careful while standing next to him.

Unraveled: Where else is he coming undone? Job? Relationships? Finances?

Worn Down: Where else is he worn down? And what's stopping him from buying a new pair of shoes?

Trendy yet Ugly: Strangely reminiscent of the *Emperor's New Clothes*. What else will this king do if he's told it's popular?

Metro-Man Shoes: Vanity alert. Date him only if you don't mind sharing your Alpha-Yin status.

Inherited Shoes: Walking in someone else's shoes? Hmmm—make sure they have some good juju.

Shoe-Shark Package Packaging Plan #2: The Bait and Switch

THE SHOES

Snazzy attention-getting shoes—on the first date. Yet watch their steady decline into the No-Approach category. Especially after you have sex with him.

THE SELL

The Bait and Switch Shoe Shark is all sizzle up front. He uses lots of conditional modal verbs about all he could be and all that you could have with him. All this fluffery is to lock you in based on his conditional potential. While it's true that Bait and Switch shoe sharks are full of potential, unfortunately they're usually full of something else too. Time will tell. And so do his shoes. When you've waited long enough for his potential to be realized, don't let him explain it away with even more conditional modal verbs. Buyers beware because when you buy a shoe shark's excuses, you don't get your money back.

Sole Story

From the moment Karyn met Will, it was attraction city. He had that goateed bad-boy look that she loved, owned his own advertising agency, and wore hot shoes that made her toes curl in anticipation. Will took Karyn on a romantic first date, stared deeply into her eyes, and told her he wanted a commitment. Karyn felt absolutely swept off her feet.

But after the first month, Will started picking her up late and only wanted to hang out—late night. His shoes changed too. Gone were the sexy Italian loafers and stylish Mark Nason boots. Hello dirty sneakers and easy bowlers. Next came the excuses and conditional modal verbs.

Will also had a five-year-old son who suddenly became the excuse for his failure to call or show up on time. When Karyn expressed her disappointment about the various upsets in their dates, Will told her "she didn't know what it was like to be a father." He said she didn't understand what he was going through, and she should be patient. After a few weeks of "patience" Karyn got fed up and moved on.

Three months later, Will called—late night. He wanted her to come over. Karyn laughed. Will was sympathetic. He said, "I know baby. It's tough. But hang in there. Things will lighten up for me soon." Karyn rolled her eyes so hard she thought they'd pop out of her head. Karyn asked if Will could hear a noise. He asked, "What noise?" Then he heard it. It was the dial tone.

Shoe-Shark Package Packaging Plan #3: The Take-Back

THE SHOES

Ultra parfait. These shoes shine, even in the dark. They are usually *very expensive.* The Take-Back Shoe Shark knows that if you see expensive shoes on his feet, you'll fantasize about him buying you the equivalent. That's his hook. His angle is to make you think that if you give him what he wants, he'll give you what you want. But that's not the way to treat a flower in the desert. On the contrary, flowers in the desert get what they want *first.*

THE SELL

The Take-Back Shoe Shark is smooth. He's a pro among professionals and does everything right. He is five minutes early with flowers at the doorstep. He may even ask if you want a big or small wedding. No conditional modal verbs roll off his tongue. Instead, they are expertly inferred. Everything he says or does is all part of his Package Packaging Plan.

Yet, after a limited amount of "extreme romance" investment, if this shoe shark doesn't get what he wants prepare for the take-back. He'll drop you as if nothing ever happened. He'll leave you high and dry, wondering what you did wrong. He promised you the world and treated you like a queen for a few dates, but when you acted like a lady, he disappeared back into the blue. The truth is that you did nothing wrong. If fact, you did everything right by wedging a pitchfork into his Package Packaging Plan.

Sole Story

As Sherrie walked across a crowded bar, a handsome man said, "Happy Birthday." Sherrie was shocked. She didn't know him. How could he have known that her birthday was only two days before? Ben admitted that he had been at the same restaurant where she had celebrated with friends. Sherrie was impressed. She felt flattered that he remembered her. She became even more interested in Ben when she saw his shoes. Classic black Prada loafers. Major points for Ben. He was just her kind of guy.

Sherrie and Ben took a cab to a mutual friend's house for an after-party at the beach. On the patio, Ben told her that the only reason he went to the party was to be with her. More points for Ben. Within the hour, Ben revealed to Sherrie that his house was conveniently only a block away. Sherrie agreed to visit but only for a moment. It was a warm evening and the moon shined down on them as they walked barefoot on the beach. Ben was racking up the points. Here was a guy who wears Prada <u>and</u> walks barefoot. Amazing.

When they arrived at Ben's house, Sherrie looked at her feet. From the walk on the beach they weren't looking so fresh. Ben ran the water in the bath. "Let me wash your feet," he said. Sherrie hesitated. "Don't worry," he said, "I'm Buddhist. It's a sign of respect." Sherrie let Ben wash her feet. It was nice to be pampered. No man had ever washed her feet before. In fact, Sherrie felt so respected that she accepted Ben's invitation to spend the night. Although Sherrie laid down the rules of engagement—which was no engagement—Ben had belated birthday sex on his mind. Soon Sherrie felt Ben's respect for her started and ended at her feet.

Sherrie got up to call herself a cab. "I thought you said you were a Buddhist," she said. Ben smiled devilishly, "I didn't say I was a good one." Two weeks later, Sherrie saw Ben at the same bar they had met at before. This time he had nothing to say to her. He was too busy giving another woman a foot massage.

Animal Instincts

While dealing with a Shoe Shark, you might want to take note of the type of skin his shoes are made of. This will give you insight into his predatory animal instincts.

Alligator: Larger males tend to be solitary territorial creatures. While smaller males tend to tolerate each other in groups for added protection. Alligators are quite opportunistic eaters. They eat everything they see, including smaller alligators. Ouch!

Crocodile: The most advanced of all reptiles; they are ambush predators waiting for prey to come near before attacking with their powerful jaws. Most experienced crocodile handlers know that a crocodile cannot open its jaws if held shut. But that's a trick in itself.

Ostrich: These top-heavy, oversized birds with twiggy legs and knobby knees eat almost everything they see—especially when in captivity. Although it isn't scientifically true, ostriches are known to put their heads in the sand at the first whiff of danger. In reality, they take a different approach by laying their necks across the sand to appear as if they have "disappeared."

Shark: One of the most stealthy predators, most of us don't see them coming before it's too late. Although most sharks let go after one bite, that alone can be lethal.

Lizard: Fickle and cold blooded, lizards are known to change color according to situational circumstances and to hiss when upset or provoked. And when held in captivity, they are notorious for making a smelly mess in the bathroom.

Bitching and Moaning

Once men know that *we* know how they package their package, they might want to embrace honesty as the best policy. In the beginning of this policy change, you can expect a little resistance. Perhaps even some bitching. Only men don't usually admit that they're bitching. Yet if a man has to change something about himself to get what he wants, prepare for him to either mope or try to convince you that they're *only* shoes.

Don't back down. And this is why: all his bitching, moaning, and moping have more to do with him than they have to do with you. This behavior is exhibited because men don't like to change. They want to get what they can—including you—for the lowest price possible. So, when you raise the bar, expect a little resistance. Men liked the days when they could excuse their crumbling sneakers with droopy laces by saying they're only shoes. They could cop a blank expression and pretend not to know.

Those days are over. Men know (that you know that they know) that their shoes express qualities of themselves you are looking for—or not—in a relationship with them. No more excuses. Anything else than a man's best foot forward is hence considered lazy.

Be strong in your *shoe convictions.* Stay firm. Don't lower your standards of the qualities you desire to see a man express through his shoes and in his relationship with you. When a man realizes that his excuses aren't working, he'll either *step up* or disappear to look for another woman who'll give him what he wants for less. You aren't a discount store. And you attract better customers if you mark up your goods.

Definitions

Shoe Convictions—*What a woman will and won't put up with concerning a man and his shoes and her relationship with him.*

Step Up—*The conscious act when a man decides to do better in the shoe aspect of life.*

MISSING LINK

So, why don't all men put their best foot forward? According to Tom Parker, former creative director for Yahoo! Personals, men dread shoe shopping because it's the only item of clothing that isn't self-service. "It's the equivalent of a man asking for directions," he says. "You have to have another person help you." He also equates buying new shoes with the equivalent joy that women approach bathing suit shopping—except without the privacy of the dressing room. "And unless it's a puffy white sneaker, the break-in process can be brutal. That's why a guy will go out and buy an entire closet of new clothes but will then go out wearing the same old cruddy shoes."

Yet, we do it. Women consistently put their best foot forward when it comes to exhibiting on the outside the qualities we want to attract a man with on the inside. And no one can argue that women's shoes are particularly comfortable. That's why women judge a man by his shoes. The effort men put into their shoes is directly proportional to the effort we anticipate they will put into the relationship. Oprah brought the point home with her famous quote, "I still have my feet on the ground. I just wear better shoes."

STEPPING UP

When a man decides to step up to the shoe plate, support him. Perhaps even give him a helping hand with style and lend a sympathetic ear. Remember, if you give a man a fish, you feed him for a day. But if you teach a man how to shop for shoes, you feed him for a lifetime.

Even the movie *Field of Dreams* touches on the sage advice of Be Do Have. Kevin Costner first had to build the field before "they" came. Life works the same way. A man first must become the kind of man the woman of his dreams would be attracted to, and then just like in the movie, she will come.

The good news is that there is a sock for every shoe. So the next time you hear a guy complaining about having to do better in the shoe department of life, remind him that he can meet the woman of his dreams simply by wearing better shoes.

That is a lot easier than building a baseball diamond in a cornfield.

Yet if a man continues to be nasty about stepping up, simply say, "Sorry, chump." Whether he likes it or not, it's happening anyway. Women have always judged a man by his shoes. And we always will. It's in our psyche. So men have a choice. Either they can be salmons and fight their way upstream or they can use this information to flow with the river and find their solemates. You decide which kind of man you want to be with. A salmon? Or a smarter sole?

A Tale of Two Fish

The Salmon

Sarah doesn't just judge a man by his shoes only for herself. She also does it for her qualifying single friends as well. When Sarah plays matchmaker, a prospective date's shoes are the clincher whether he gets passed on or passed by. Sarah met Scott at a swank BBQ. After several minutes of conversation, she thought he might be the perfect match for her friend. They both loved dogs. They both listened to the same obscure DJ mixes. And they lived only a few miles away from each other.

There were a few more items Sarah checked off from her girlfriend's man list. Scott was attractive, well traveled, charming, and rich. He seemed like he was going for it all. But when Sarah's eyes fell on his shoes, she winced and shook her head sadly. His look (pressed khaki shorts, matching belt, stylish polo shirt, and orange sweater) was totally incongruent with his shoes—worn-out, dirty, Velcro river walkers. Even though the shoes were the one and only out, there would be no setup.

Sarah mentally perused the list of her attractive single friends who might overlook such an indiscretion. None came to mind. In the matter of a minute, unknown to him, Scott was instantly blackballed from a long list of attractive available women because of his unfortunate lack of attention to his footwear. In the same unit of time it would have taken Scott to make a better choice in footwear, he was banned from Sarah's network of hot friends. Sarah didn't feel bad about her choice. In fact, she would have liked nothing more than to attend Scott's wedding with one of her amazing friends. But there would be no introductions because Sarah already knew that her friends would also wince and walk away.

A Smarter Sole

Sunshine's boyfriend, Chip, grew up with three sisters and understood at an early age just how important shoes were. In fact, he skillfully uses the concepts of Soleology to his advantage at work. Chip is a producer in the entertainment business in Hollywood and knows how important it is to present the right aspect of himself to the right people to seal the deal. While making business decisions, he knows that the other parties are looking for people just like themselves who they can feel comfortable working with.

Before he gets dressed for any meeting, Chip calls Sunshine for a shoe consultation. She always asks him the same questions: (1) Who is he meeting? (2) What's the purpose of the meeting? (3) Where are they meeting? Since Chip has a selection of shoes from rugged urban construction boots to hoochie Gucci "gold chain" loafers, he can play any part. Sunshine knows every shoe Chip owns and expertly pairs them to the exact purpose he wants to get out of the meeting. Sunshine feels like she's found the ultimate man. Not only do they have intelligent conversations, but they have intelligent conversations about shoes.

CHAPTER 11

Sole Returns

Sole Note:

What a man invests in his shoes, you get back in the relationship.

Since time is the most valuable asset we own, we do our best to save it. Yet while trying to save time, we can't help but spend it. Which is just how slippery time is. And if we did save it, where would we put it? Rather than saving time, invest it. Because with any good investment, there will be a return. For example, if you invest $1,000 annually at 10 percent interest, you'll have $198,393 in thirty years. Not bad. When investing time in money, compound interest is your friend.

But what about our relationships? Aren't we supposed to invest our time in a man? Doesn't a kiss turn a frog into a prince? Not when you consider *the Principle of Investment.* If the frog is a frog, no amount of kissing—even Big Red style—will turn him into a prince. Instead, when you open your eyes, you'll be surrounded by even more frogs puckering up for a kiss.

Before you make another investment in a man, whether it's your time, money, your youth, or your heart, take a close look at his *Investment Principal.* Be careful not to confuse the Principle of Investment with your Investment Principal. They are two entirely different animals. The difference between meeting the solemate of your dreams and kissing frogs forever lies in your understanding between these two concepts.

Definitions

The Principle of Investment—*The universal law that states whatever you invest your time and attention in grows.*

Investment Principal—*The very thing that you invest your time and attention in that grows but never changes from its original self.*

The Principle of Investment works fabulously well with money because you want more of your Investment Principal. Whether you invest one month or thirty years of your time in your Investment Principal, theoretically you get more of what you started with. You don't expect your dollars to change into anything else but more dollars. If they did, you'd really be disappointed because your goal of investing time in your money was to get more money.

What about men? Aren't we supposed to invest our time in a man? Let's take a vote. How many of us invested our time in a man thinking that after *X* number of years he'd change into what we wanted him to be? Then when he didn't change, we still didn't end the relationship because by then we were so pissed off that we were willing to wait some more to get our just deserts. We think, how could I have put in *X* number of years into the relationship and not received what I wanted? Well, the truth is that we did receive our just deserts. It just wasn't what we wanted or expected because the return on our investment was more of the original Investment Principal—which was the very thing we were hoping to change. Oops.

The Way to Work It: Your Investment Principal

In the relationship game, we are all shaking it, working it, and selling ourselves. Everyone is looking for the maximum return on the minimum investment. Yet, one of the biggest bones women have to pick with men is follow-through—or lack thereof. Men can be great at selling the sizzle and sealing the deal. But when it comes to delivery, something happens at the warehouse, and you don't always get what you ordered. Then we fall into the trap of waiting for that "great guy" we invested our time in to come back and give us our just return. When we don't get our expected return on our Investment Principal our minds may fill with excuses such as he's *just* been through so much or he *just* got out of a relationship. Yet imagine for a minute that instead of a man, you invested in a toaster oven. You were all excited about it. It had all the right parts and the look you loved, but when you got it home, the damn thing didn't work. What do you do? Make excuses for the manufacturer, "They *are just* going through so much right now"? Do you give it more time to start working because it *just* came out of the box?

Nope. You'd return it, exchange it, toss it, or buy a better one. You wouldn't keep it around thinking that after *X* number of years, it would eventually turn into a blender. You wouldn't continue to invest your time in a toaster oven that wasn't working. Nor would you invest in a toaster oven when you wanted a blender. So, why do it with a man?

Before you invest your time *in* a man, use his shoes to consider his Investment Principal. Factor in your sole impression and your answers to the four Pre-Relationship Questions (see

p. 59). That way you won't invest your time in a man wearing a matching soft beige suede shoe and sweater twinset when you're really looking for someone more adventurous in leather.

If you invest in a Vans man thinking that you'll get Kenneth Cole after five years, chances are you'll be frustrated by your return of investment. This is because Principals of Investment only change because of *outside market forces.* Barring a natural disaster or the apocalypse, the probability is that after *X* amount of years invested, there'll be more Vans in your man than you ever thought possible. That is why it's so important that your Investment Principal is your heart's desire from the get-go. Because whatever it is, inevitably you'll get more of it than you ever bargained for.

Definition

Outside Market Forces—*Outside circumstances that pressurize a man into facilitating change. A classic outside market force is "The Marriage Ultimatum."*

Money Honey

When we don't get what we want out of a relationship, sometimes we start making excuses for a man's lousy sole profile or getting sucked into a Shoe Shark's No-Approach Package Packaging Plan. The most common excuse is that he "just doesn't have much money right now." Okay, a trip to Paris might be out of the question, but how about a decent pair of shoes? An even better question to ask is, Why isn't he making much money right now? Is he doing all he can with everything he has and putting his best foot forward?

If we make excuses for a man's lousy choice in shoes, we give him a "Get Out of Jail Free" Card. Once you start giving those away, you've just flushed down the toilet any incentive for a man to change and do better. Besides, why should he change when he is already enjoying all the benefits of a relationship with you without doing any of the heavy lifting? This is what your mother meant by giving the milk away for free. The milk is your time and your attention. Don't give it away for free.

Consider Soleology a zero-tolerance, excuse-free zone. No amount of explaining can excuse less than best-foot-forward intentions in men's shoes. When you excuse men for their unattractive choices in their footwear, you're cheating yourself from meeting the solemate of your dreams. Excuses are like ripples in a pond. They proliferate. If you excuse your man's lack of approach, most likely you'll make excuses for his other less-than-attractive choices in other areas of your relationship too.

Sole Story

Barbara first met Gunther, an artist in New York, when he barely had two pennies to rub together. But Gunther decided that he would never be a starving artist. Gunther borrowed money from Barbara and invested his last dime in a pair of amazing Budapest shoes he bought on e-Bay. They were easily recognizable with their signature contrasting colors and winged derby cap. Rather than slave away for years as an assistant, Gunther wanted to be on the fast track to fame. He knew these shoes would be his ticket into the exclusive and elusive SoHo art scene.

When he caught wind of a must-see-and-be-seen party, Gunther walked there until the last block, then he hailed a cab and rode the last three hundred feet. He climbed out of the taxi like a rock star, feet first. Gunther didn't say much to the doorman. Instead, he let his shoes do the talking. Although the doorman had no idea who Gunther was, he immediately let him in. If he was wearing Budapest shoes, he must be somebody.

Once inside, the shoes created even more of a stir because an artist wearing master craftsman European shoes, imported from the banks of the Danube, must have already entertained some level of success. When he spoke about his art, people listened. Gunther's shoes worked the art scene like no other. Soon, he had stirred up enough interest in his art that a small gallery hosted his first show. Literally, Gunther's cunning selection of shoes got him his first foot in the door.

The Soleology Investment Principal Work Sheet

First answer the four *Pre*relationship questions below to be clear on whether or not you want to accrue compound interest on his Investment Principal.

1. Who is he *really?*
2. How does he feel about himself *really?*
3. What can you expect from him in a relationship *really?*
4. What can you expect from him in a relationship *in bed?*

Now, use your answers above to determine the value of his Investment Principal.

5. I am satisfied with ____ percent of his total Investment Principal.
6. I would like to change ____ percent

Based on my answers, his Investment Principal (circle one) is/isn't worth investing my time and attention into a relationship with him.

PART FOUR

The You in His Shoe

The good news about being in a relationship is that it lets us experience more of our self than we ever could alone. That's why your attraction reactions are so important. Like a good friend, they give you a push toward a good fit to try to pull you away from getting pinched. Rather than being a leaf in the wind drifting on random currents of circumstance, you want to learn how to create your own good luck—especially when it comes to finding the solemate of your dreams.

You see, fairy tales don't tell you the whole story. In fact, they leave out a very important lesson. Happy endings don't just magically appear. They usually take some behind-the-scenes work before Prince Charming is charmed. Just like a ballerina appears to glide effortlessly across the stage, it actually takes continual practice, determination, and strength to appear so light and elegant. Rather than waiting for the summer wind to blow Prince Charming your way, you must first create room in your life for him to show up. Second, you must believe he will. Then as if by magic, he does.

Yet, there's more to this magical formula. What Disney doesn't tell you about fairy tales is that moments before Prince Charming shows up—our soon-to-be princess has already spent the better half of the movie practicing determination and strength. She hasn't settled for less. Even in the face of adversity she said no to what she didn't want. She held herself together and never stopped believing that she would live in that castle on the hill. Her fortitude is the magical beauty that sweeps a prince off his feet and in turn inspires him to sweep you off yours.

CHAPTER 12

Never Met a Bad Shoe

Sole Quote:

"Shoes are at the top of the pecking order of a man's ensemble." —Allan Flusser

When you find yourself attracted to a man *and* his shoes, that's a big green light to go forward into a relationship. Yet, what do you do when you like him but his shoes are a cause for alarm? Regardless of the apparent confusion, this is actually good news. First of all, there's no such thing as a bad shoe. We are the ones who put the "good" or "bad" label on men's shoes depending on how we judge our experience with their particular owners. Whether or not you're attracted to them is a different story. Ultimately, it's always our decision what to do—or not do—about the signs a man's shoes offer us, which is why it's totally inappropriate to blame the shoe. It's not the shoe's fault the owner didn't know they went out of style in the 1980s and should have been given a proper burial.

When deciding which lucky men we date, all men's shoes are our friends. Especially, the shoes we don't like. Perhaps they're his wicker Man Sandals, smelly thongs, or tasseled moccasin backless slip-on loafers with a leather weave top. In fact, it's always the "worst" shoes that give us the best information. They're like that one special friend who will always tell you if you have food in your teeth or if you do look fat in that dress. So please don't shoot the messenger. Listen to the messenger instead. Men's shoes are only trying to save you from unnecessary spontaneous relationship combustion.

At some point in your relationships, you will find yourself in a distasteful man/shoe experience. The underlying cause is usually one of three things: (1) It's a Style Issue: and the polar opposite of yours. (2) It's Him: his shoes reflect something you don't like about him. (3) It's You: his shoes reflect something you don't like about yourself. First, let's take a look at the simplest and easiest to fix.

I Don't Like His Shoes

REASON #1: STYLE ISSUE

This is the one place in Soleology where men can be given a little leeway and a helping hand. Perhaps his shoes are well kept and clean, and there's nothing really wrong with them except (insert horror music here) they're absolutely hideous. Usually, the culprit is an ex-girlfriend who went wild for his shoes and told him that she was hot for them—in the eighties. Since then, they've become a permanent part of his Package Packaging Plan. In which case, your man needs not only a style lesson but a calendar as well.

As much as women try to be "nice," there are some shoes that we just can't do. Ever. So, if you're feeling that you just can't get over "the shoe thing," don't feel that you're being small or petty. Bad shoes are up there with bad toupees. It's okay not to be attracted to a man's shoes. And in some cases, it's better that you aren't. This can be a very good lesson for any man. When it comes to his shoes, a man's Package Packaging Plan should be updated seasonally. So, if it's not his bad breath that is keeping you from getting closer but his personal taste in footwear, try one of these four Attraction Complication Fixer-Uppers.

1. *Be Direct.* Tell him you'd be more attracted to him if you picked out his shoes. Then let him do *the math.*

Definition

The Math—*Anything that when increased, proportionally increases a man's chance of sex.*

2. *Be Indirect.* Discretely introduce new shoes as gifts on birthdays, holidays, anniversaries, and any other holiday you can think of or invent.
3. *Positive Reinforcement.* Give kudos and rewards when he wears attractive shoes. If the rewards are memorable, guaranteed he'll wear those shoes again.
4. *Cement Boots.* Facilitate change. If you're desperate, the offensive shoes can suddenly somehow, mysteriously disappear.

Sole Story

Liila had been dating Mark for almost three months. Things were going really well. He treated her fabulously, and there was some real magic happening between them. Yet, there was just one "little" thing Liila couldn't wrap her head around. She hated a particular pair of smooth black leather, gaucho-style, zip-up ankle boots that he wore on almost every date. Every time he wore those boots, Liila could barely keep her food down. She thought they made his feet look too dainty under his massive build.

After a few months of painfully enduring the boots, the words finally burst out of her mouth, "I hate your shoes." Mark shrugged coolly. "Why didn't you say so?" he asked. "You were always staring at them, so I thought that you liked them." The next day they went shopping together for a new pair of shoes for Mark. A year later, they got married. Liila has been happily shopping for Mark's shoes ever since.

DR. SOLE

Q. *I'm dating a guy, and we both find his shoes unattractive. What does that mean?*

A. This is a very interesting situation. You don't like his shoes. He doesn't like them either. Why then is he wearing them? Your mind might fill with excuses: money, his job, his mother. He could be wearing rentals in a wedding or be dressed like a clown for charity. Yet, if this is a habit and he isn't the captain of his own shoes, let alone his own ship, you might want to do some Awareness Expansion and see where else he let go of the reins. This is an important aspect of Soleology because when people don't outwardly express who they are, it constricts not only their sole but also their soul. It's the same feeling as having amazing news, but you're not allowed to tell anyone. Or a horse bucking at the gate ready to run, but it's locked. A plane on the runway ready to fly, but no clearance for takeoff. Shall I go on? □

Since you aren't supposed to judge someone until you walk a mile in their shoes, judging them by the shoes they choose to walk a mile in is the next best thing. If you encounter a man who doesn't like his own shoes, before you put this in the I'll Think About It Later Pile, first put his shoes on the other foot. Yours. It's important you discover for yourself what it's like to wear shoes that don't express who you are. To understand its implications fully, you'll have to walk in shoes that you don't like either.

Go to your favorite shoe store and try on the most amazing shoes you see. Circle the floor and notice how you walk and how you feel. Perhaps you feel sexy, confident, and powerful. Perhaps you feel comfortable, secure, and taken care of. Take note of whatever feelings you experience wearing shoes you adore.

Now, do the opposite. Take a trip to your least favorite shoe store. You know, the one your mom made you go to as a kid or the one where you had to buy shoes for a job that you hated. Pick out a pair of shoes that represents you the least—the complete opposite of who you are. Circle the store and notice how you walk. Watch your body language. Do you walk tall in these shoes or do you shrink and disappear? How do you feel? Ridiculous? Do the shoes itch? How long do they last on your feet before you want to scream and fling them across the room?

Now that you've walked a mile—or at least a few circles on the showroom floor—in shoes that you don't like, imagine what is slowly happening to a man who does this to himself all day, every day. Since the world we live in doesn't stand still, if we're not moving forward, we're falling behind. Every moment that you compromise yourself, even with just your shoes, you fall further behind until you realize that you're stuck in a rut and the world is so far ahead you're afraid you might never catch up.

If you're considering investing your time and attention in a man who doesn't even like his own shoes, a question to ask yourself is, What am I more interested in? Moving forward in life or being in a relationship with a man who is falling behind?

REASON #2: IT'S HIM

Something about your date's choice in footwear brings up a point that doesn't sit too well in the attraction department. Instantly, you get the vibe that an aspect of him isn't going to mesh too well with another aspect of you. It could be a pair of black Velcro sneakers, urban orange kick abouts, or green velvet flip-flops that tip you off. Perhaps his gleaming chestnut tasseled loafers are just *too* corporate? In either case, it actually matters less what the shoes are than what aspect of them rubs against your silky smooth psyche like a scratchy steel wool sweater.

To find the answer, first look deeply into his shoes and let your mind wander. And if it isn't a private moment—meaning if he's actually there—remember to keep your shoe face because it could take a minute before the answer becomes clear. If the answer doesn't suddenly jump out at you in flashing neon lights, it's time to go down the Soleological Rabbit Hole where all things shoe—past, present, and future—are known. Once down the Rabbit Hole, it's important to know that things might get a little messy for a while before they get better. Just like reorganizing your closet—the mess gets worse before it starts to feel better. So, trust yourself. And trust the process. You'll get where you want to go. The quickest and gentlest way to get there is to follow the *Soleological bread crumb trail* by clustering.

Definition

The Soleological Bread Crumb Trail—*A trail of clues that leads you back to the moment when you developed a judgment about a certain type of men's shoe.*

Soleology Exercise

It's Him! Soleological Rabbit Hole Cluster Exercise

Start with a blank piece of paper and write down everything you find unattractive about your man's shoes. Keep going until you've covered every single scratch, itch, and hitch in your psyche. In these moments, don't be surprised if your Doubting Daisy suddenly pops up with some logical reason why this is ridiculous and you shouldn't do it. In fact, now is a great time to send her on another luxurious tropical vacation. Because when you're down the Soleological Rabbit Hole, this is no time to be listening to your Doubting Daisy.

Don't be surprised if you write down more things on the page than you originally thought you had a beef with. This is entirely normal. The first time you do this exercise, it's like taking your finger out of the dam. There might have been more issues with his shoes that you were holding inside than you realized.

Once you feel like you've emptied the well, draw three lines next to each beef you wrote down about his shoes. On each of these three lines, write what that quality represents to you. Perhaps you don't like how his laces are always untied and flop about. That might represent laziness to you. And you hate laziness. Your last boyfriend was lazy and . . .

Good. You're halfway down the Soleological Rabbit Hole. In fact, the first two bits were just the prep work for what is going to happen next. First, you wrote down the elements that you found unattractive in his shoes. Then you discovered what qualities they represented to you in your life. Now, go deep to discover why those qualities bothered you.

This last step is where The Rabbit Hole can start to feel a little scary. Yet, think of it like one of those trust-building exercises where you let someone blindfold you and walk you around the room. Or you close your eyes and fall backwards into a group of waiting arms. The Soleological Rabbit Hole might look bottomless. It isn't. There is a reason why a certain aspect of his shoes bothers you. Go there. Find it. Discover what it is.

REASON #3: IT'S ME!

No book would be complete without a steamy tell-all confession. Here it is—just like Rome, all roads lead back to you. That's the ultimate truth. Even when you think it's about him—or his shoes—it's not. It's really about you. It always has been and always will be. The very "thing" that you don't like about his shoes reflects the same thing you haven't come to peace with within yourself. Otherwise, you wouldn't have reacted to his shoes. They would have remained a nonissue.

In fact, how you react toward a man's shoes tells you more than you ever thought about which way you are moving in life, which is usually one of two directions. We find ourselves moving either toward something desirable or away from something undesirable. When a man's shoes make you squirm, they represent the qualities in your life that you are trying to move away from. Perhaps these are the exact qualities about a man that you vowed to *never again* let into your life. Yet, when we are in our *never again mode*, usually we experience exactly what we don't want again and again. This is because even though you are moving away from it, *it* is still your focus, which means it will keep showing up in your life.

That's why finding a pair of men's shoes that fit not only him but also you is infinitely important. When your man's shoes make your heart sing, that's a green light for moving in the direction of your dreams, and he's a part of it. When you trust your sole impression, it means that you're captain of your own life and you trust yourself to steer it in the direction of inspiration, freedom, and love.

Sole Story

Maria remembers it like it was yesterday. That's just how much it bothered her. Steve, a date of hers, wore wingtips to the beach—on a Saturday. They were well made and expensive, but she found them troublingly boring, rigid, and confining. They were so out of place at the beach it made her wriggle in her seat at lunch. Then Steve asked Maria to walk down the boardwalk with him and hold hands. She cringed. There was no way she would be seen with a man who wore wingtips to the beach. Maria hurried the date along to an early end. Only once she was alone inside her apartment could she relax.

Maria realized her negative reactions to Steve's shoes were much too strong for her to ignore. She wanted to know exactly why they bothered her so much. After a moment of reflection, Maria wasn't surprised to realize that the words she used to describe Steve's shoes—boring, rigid, confined—were the same words she used to describe her last relationship, which she stayed in two years past its expiration date. Maria forgave herself for staying in that relationship so long, and she also forgave herself for projecting her past woes onto her unsuspecting date.

The next day, Maria called Steve to give him another chance and suggested that he might wear some flip-flops on their next outing to the beach. Steve was happy to oblige and on their next date, Maria was thrilled to hold his hand.

You see, every time you catch your sole impression, it's an invitation to get to know yourself better. If fact, it goes a little bit like this:

> Dear Me,
>
> I have been cordially invited to get to know myself better. Evidently the issues of *X*, *X*, and *X* have been reflected and brought up to my conscious mind by a certain man's shoes.
>
> Anyhoodle, I am now offered two choices about what to do—or not do—about the elements reflected in his shoes that I haven't reconciled within myself. Either (1) I can release my fear of *X*, *X*, and *X* and start living the life of my dreams or (2) I can ignore it and continue to be bugged every time men's shoes represent *X*, *X*, *X*.
>
> As always, the choice is mine.
>
> Love and Toodles,
>
> My Wonderful Mirror, a.k.a. Men's Shoes
>
> P.S. I can't tell you what to do, but when you let your fears go, there's an amazing party afterward. And the dip is out of this world.

Soleology's Attraction Rx, Part 2

While you're down *in* the Soleological Rabbit Hole, a golden opportunity awaits you. Not only are you given the chance to get to know yourself better, but also you're given the opportunity to let go of all the men and their shoes that you regret letting walk into (or walk on) your life. Write down each of their names and explain what their shoes represent to you. Did you find their shoes too harsh, mean, jagged, rough, preppy, flimsy, or stiff? What was it about them that let you down, made you doubt yourself, or broke your heart? Who are the men in your life whom you trusted at first, only to get chomped by their alligator loafers later on?

It's important to get it all down on paper, because once you let it out, you can let it go. Keep some tissues nearby and a jumbo bar of your favorite chocolate. Go ahead—think of all the men who have hurt you, wronged you, and misled you. Think of all the men's shoes that you hated but let walk into your life anyway. As you think about them, thank them. They were only in your life to teach you who you want to be in *relation*ship to them. Perhaps, they were here to teach you what you don't want so that now you can move in the direction of what you do want.

Once you know what you were meant to learn, release their tenancy and let them go. Because when we aren't holding on to what we don't want, we make room for the solemate of our dreams to step in. This is the man who will make your sole impression jump for joy, and you'll have that wondrous "this is it!" tingle from head to toe.

The Big Brown Shopping Bag of Life

When you're ready to let go, you might be wondering, How do I do it? You now understand that all of your hopes, fears, and dreams are reflected back to you through your reactions to men's shoes. So, you're halfway there. Now you want to release whatever it is that is holding you back from meeting the solemate of your dreams. The first step to take is simply to decide to do it. This may seem overly elemental, but letting go is actually one of the most powerful decisions you can make in your life. Our sheer intention has the power to make everything new. Anything else is simply for ceremonial purposes only. Yet, ceremonies can be fun. And they can also strengthen your intention. So let the ceremonies begin!

The second step to clear out the past is to have a nice long look into your Big Brown Shopping Bag of Life. This is something we all carry with us. It's our "baggage." Having baggage isn't necessarily a bad thing; it just depends on what you fill it up with.

Each of us carries around a Big Brown Shopping Bag of Life, and we can fill it with anything that we want. The only glitch is that the bag is only so big. Just like there are only twenty-four hours in a day, there's not enough room for everything in our shopping bags. We must pick and choose what we decide to put into our Big Brown Shopping Bag of Life. Imagine that you are shopping at the most fabulous shoe store in Paris. Every pair of shoes is for your taking. Yet, you can only put in so many pairs before your bag is full. So what do you do? You have two choices:

Option One: Fill your Big Brown Shopping Bag with shoes that you don't like, that hurt, or that don't fit well.

Option Two: Fill your Big Brown Shopping Bag with shoes that you adore, that you feel comfortable in, and that express your personality.

You should take this opportunity to get to know yourself better. Open up your Big Brown Bag Shopping Bag of Life and have a look inside. Is your bag filled with "No! I hate these shoes" or "Yes! These are amazing shoes"? It's amazing how many women fill their Big Brown Shopping Bags of Life with not only shoes but also relationships that don't fit. This is because many women were taught how important it is to be nice. And being nice didn't include anything as *unpleasant* as the word *no.* Yet, this is a very important word because what we say *no* to actually creates our *yes.* For example, if you say no to a Shoe Shark's Bait and Switch Package Packaging Plan, you then create the space Mr. All the Right Shoes to waltz into your life. Remember, your solemate can't ask you to dance if your dance card is already full.

Being in a relationship is like playing cards. When you've got an Ace, you don't want to give it away for a two. Filling your Big Brown Shopping Bag of Life with what you don't want is the equivalent of exchanging your Ace for his two, which means you'll probably be too busy squabbling with your two that doesn't fit to notice when your Ace of a solemate walks by.

Since what you say no to creates your yes, Soleology offers a few fun ways to practice saying that magical two-letter word first in the privacy of your own home. Pretend for a moment that you're a famous actress and your big part is coming up. You only have one line, but it's the most important moment in the whole movie. When the male lead—a Shoe Shark—offers you his red-flag Package Packaging Plan, the fate of the entire movie depends on your amazing delivery of this small but mighty word—No.

The most famous female leads wouldn't think of performing without practicing their part. Schedule a rehearsal with yourself in front of the mirror to practice your line. No. No. No. Say it all different ways. No way. Not on your life! Don't even think about it! Say it with a smile, a hair flip, or even a curtsey. Or if you're feeling saucy, try an over-the-shoulder no. Practice your line until the word rolls off your tongue. Imagine all the men's shoes you would say no to. Line them up in your mind and just like ticking off a shopping list—tell each of them thank you for your consideration, but no!

If for whatever reason, a not-so gentleman isn't taking no for your answer, simply *pull a princess.* Because a princess always sits on her throne—even if it's on the subway, cast your eyes down on the peasant and say the words, "How dare you! Which syllable of *no* did you not understand." And if he retorts, "You're such a *princess*" (like it's a bad thing!) lower your eyes even more and say "Of course, I am." Besides, that is certainly no way to treat the female lead. He's fired! Off the set! Next!

Definition

Pull a Princess—*The sudden transformation of yourself into royalty and the expectation to be treated as such.*

Whatever you find in your Big Brown Shopping Bag of Life, there's no reason to worry or work yourself up about it. Einstein was right—space is neither created nor destroyed. It's used. And how we use it is up to us. Saying *no* to what we don't want makes room for what we do want. It's the same space. Only we decide to fill our life with rocks or rockets. And when it comes to creating space, there's a Soleology Rx that is really easy: simply take out everything that doesn't belong in your Big Brown Shopping Bag of Life and replace it with something you like better. It's a bit like dumping out your Halloween candy bag as a kid. You quickly weeded out all the icky hard candy and pennies and kept all the prime goodies for yourself. Why then did we ever stop doing that?

CHAPTER 13

From the Sole Up

Sole Note:

When his shoes have it, you know he's on the good foot.

In relationships with men, there are no right or wrong shoes. And there are no right or wrong reactions. There is only your reaction. And it's always right. No matter what it looks like or how it feels, just as with men's shoes—every relationship is really about you. Relationships are like mirrors. The real reason we become involved with another person, place, or thing is so that we can see ourselves better through our relationship with it. We have different relationships that reflect different aspects of ourselves back to us. Which is why men's shoes contain all the answers you need in your romantic relationships. Your attraction reactions to a man's shoes are really a reflection of yourself that says, "Right back at you baby!"

As you become a Soleological Master remember that relationships exist so that you can decide who you want to be in relationship to yourself, your man, his shoes, your family, your friends, your coworkers, your neighbors, their shoes, your pets, your plants, your home, your car, and so forth. Relationships are a cosmic wall that you bounce your thoughts, ideas, and actions against. Relationships allow you to decide how you want to play the relationship game. Will you be a team player? Have fun with it? Low ball? Hog the ball? Play fair? Play dirty? Quit? Or aim high and expect to win? Men—and their shoes—show up in your life to help you play. You can't do it alone. It takes two to win.

Classically, while trying to understand another person, we're told to imagine ourselves walking in his or her shoes. That is what actors, artists—and writers—have been doing for millennia. They profit creatively from the insight that a man's shoes are characteristic of his persona. These artists build their characters from the sole up, first by imagining the shoes their characters would wear and, also, by imagining the shoes their characters would never wear. It's from the character's sole that the persona emerges. One could call this Soleology's Trickle *Up* Theory.

Definition

Trickle Up Theory—*Building a character's persona from the sole up.*

In life, actors aren't the only ones who can benefit from Soleology's Trickle Up Theory. We are all building personas. We are all playing roles. That is why changing your life can be as simple as changing your shoes. The only obstacle you may have to this is resistance to change.

Sole Story

Kimiko remembers the day she'd finally had it with David. His attitude was just as uptight as his shoes. She was ready to throw both of them out. In their last fight, Kimiko found herself saying, "You're just like your shoes!" She had a descriptive laundry list of how his shoes were no fun, terribly boring, and totally predictable. To her surprise a tear ran down David's cheek. "You're right," he said. David tore into their bedroom and didn't come out for several hours.

What Kimiko discovered was that he was sitting on the floor in their bedroom facing the closet and his shoes. David told her that as he looked at each shoe, he could hear all these voices from his past telling him what to do. David said he could hear his mother say, "You'd better keep those because they were expensive." He could feel resistance giving away a pair of cap toe wingtips his Dad had given him for his first job interview in a field he never even wanted to be in.

David grabbed a grocery bag and tossed out every pair of shoes that weren't entirely him. When he was done with his sole purge, he was left with two pairs. Kimiko joined in and found herself giving away two bags full of shoes that had nothing to do with who she was or wanted to be. The next day the two of them went shopping together for shoes that fit them just right and had more fun that day than they could each remember.

Definition

Sole Purge—*The release of old shoes and old attachments that no longer serve you.*

How badly is your man in need of a sole purge?

Dire
Desperate
Major overhaul
Could use some renovation
A little tweaking
Attuned
At peace with his sole

Tell Me What You Want—What You Really, Really Want

When it comes to romantic relationships, it's not only the Spice Girls who get what they want—you can too. Art doesn't just happen by itself. Neither do relationships. Just like an artist, create what you want from the sole up. When you do that, you increase your chances of getting it by the millions. Don't just let men and their shoes happen to you. Make it happen for you.

So, what do you want in a man? How do you want to see those traits expressed through his shoes? What is it about men's shoes that makes you want to *shoop?* Write it down. Explore every detail. Every nook and cranny. Every sole. Create for yourself the perfect pair of shoes, that if you were a shoe, you would fall in love with. What do these shoes look like? Feel like? How does he wear them? Where does he wear them? How do they rub up against your skin? How do they walk? Where do they take you? What are they made of? How long will they last? You don't have to stop at one pair. Create the perfect menagerie of shoes that you want to see on your solemate's feet. What shoes does he wear to work and at play? What's his archetype? What shoes does he wear to take you out for a night of romance?

Now, that we've got his sole worked out, let the aspects of his shoes and what they represent to you trickle up to the man himself. Who is the man who walks in these dreamy shoes? Describe him. What are his characteristics? Create for yourself your very own Super*Hot* Sexy Loverman from the sole up. What are his looks, talents, and tendencies? How does he play the relationship game? What is his sense of adventure? His taste? How many dimples? Where? What is his style? What are his quirks? How do his eyelashes curl?

Pretend you're a kid sitting on Santa's lap. This is no time to be shy. Ask for it all. Have fun and play as you create your very own Super*Hot* Sexy Loverman. Draw a picture. Cut one out of a magazine. Write down every quality, nuance, and characteristic you've ever dreamed of experiencing in a man and his shoes. Be as specific as how many hairs you want on his head to how he holds you when you sleep.

Now, describe your relationship with him. What aspects of yourself do you want to express through your relationship with him? Do you want to be adventurous or artistic or tender and trusting? Do you want to be settled, secure, and sweet? Or do you want to be wild, spontaneous, and unpredictable? How will you express more of yourself in your relationship? And what will you reflect back to each other?

As you write, don't edit yourself. Let your words flow. You might be surprised at what comes out of you that you never knew was there before. It's also a good idea to make sure your Doubting Daisy is vacationing far, far away before you begin. You certainly don't need her to give you any flack about learning all you can about yourself so that you will know what you want to express about yourself in a relationship. And if she does, just tell her that in a restaurant the cooks don't know what you want until you put in an order.

DR. SOLE

Q. *I always find something wrong with a man's shoes. Is this normal?*

A. It's important to remember that there is no such thing as the perfect shoe. If women were already perfect, we wouldn't need men or their shoes; relationships; Soleology; or chocolate. Bring it back to yourself. It's not about whether you like his shoes. It's about expressing ourselves to the greatest degree that we can through the men we choose to be with. Relationships with men allow us to express more of ourselves than we ever could alone. Rather than looking for the perfect shoe, look for a man who wears shoes that let you express more of who you are than you ever could by yourself. Ultimately, that is the goal in relationships. □

The Moment of Truth

You've built the solemate of your dreams. You know all about him—including the shoes he wears—and the relationship you want with him in vivid color. Now is a good time to see how your date, boyfriend, husband, lover, or love interest measures up to what you want to experience in a man and your relationship with him. It's time to take out his sole profile and put it side by side with your Super*Hot* Sexy Loverman wish list.

How does your man stand up? Did you just describe him? Are there a few wibbles and wobbles? Or are you exhausting yourself trying to shove a circle into a square? Only you know the answer. You and your intuition. Whatever answer you come up with—just like there are no bad shoes—there is no bad news. This is because you are closer than you ever have been before to having the solemate of your dreams. Now that you know exactly what you want—you can ask for it.

Ladies, don't judge a man by his shoes so that you can anticipate his next move in the relationship. Instead, redirect the spotlight on you! The reason you discover the Soul of his Sole is to decide if the shoe fits. Who? You! Judging a man by his shoes is more like a fact-finding mission to decide if you like what you found. Then you can ask yourself the question: Is this a shoe I can live with? Is this a shoe I want to share my life with? So, don't try to climb inside a man's head. Climb inside yours instead. Everything you ever wanted to know is already there.

During moments of truth, expect your Doubting Daisy to try to rattle your brain with her best excuses why it's impossible to find your solemate. Do not be rattled. Do not put on your Truth Protection Suit. Or high kick the truth far, far away. Your Doubting Daisy has a mute button. Press it. Because the truth is that you can get what you want. All of it! And the truth is that your Doubting Daisy doesn't know about how attraction works. The good news is that you are about to.

How Do You Get What You Want? (What You Really, Really Want)

What if you haven't found the solemate of your dreams? What if you're in a relationship already, and you find that you're shoving a circle into a square? Does this mean that the relationship is over? Au contraire. Unless, of course, you want it to be. Before you give up hope of finding the solemate of your dreams or calling it quits with your current beau, try this: Use the very thing that brought you two together to your advantage. Attraction. Only this time, make it work for you.

Every minute of every day, we're given a chance to make everything new. We only have to say yes. To do this, don't focus on where you came from—concentrate instead on where you're headed. Whatever mistakes you made learning your lessons in the romance department of life was just a chapter in the book you had to read to get a Masters in the Art of Creating Your Own Happiness. Most of us don't even remember what we learned in college, but we hang onto the love lessons that hurt us the most. But those were yesterday's *news*. Today you're taking a step in a brand-new direction, which means nothing can be the same. When you're focused on the fabulous future you envision for yourself, the very things you dream of will start to dream of you. Then each day you step forward, your dreams will take ten steps forward to find you. Until one day—and it's inevitable—you will meet.

As you go out with your newfound shoe consciousness, remember that there are Doubting Daisies among us. Some live in our head. Others live in the next room. Anytime you introduce something new to the world, the welcome wagon may not be so welcome. Instead, it can be filled with fear, skepticism, and doubt.

Soleology is no different. Some might scoff. Toss their heads in indignation. Or—even worse—try to tell you that it's petty or superficial to judge a man by his shoes. But they haven't read this book. They don't understand. Doubting Daisies are afraid of what they don't understand. Don't let that stop you. Thoughts are as flimsy as fashion. They go in and out of style. What the world calls crazy one year is praised as genius the next. Guess what? You're a genius.

Imagine if:

Mother Teresa
Oprah
Margaret Thatcher
Harriet Tubman
J. K. Rowling
Rhonda Byrne
Arianna Huffington
Maria Montessori
Princess Diana
Lisa Nichols
Rosa Parks
Susan B. Anthony
Shonda Rhimes
Dr. Pat Allen
Anne Frank
Joan of Arc
Aung San Suu Kyi
Madeleine L'Engle

Angela Merkel
Jane Addams
Mae West
Bertha Von Suttner
Sojouner Truth
Florence Scovel Shinn
Hillary Clinton
Florence Nightingale
Jillian Alexander
Sonia Gandhi
Jane Austen
Emily Green Balch
Alva Myrdal
Betty Williams
Lisa Randall
Mairead Corrigan
Rigoberta Menchú
Jody Williams
Joan Sozio
Shirin Ebadi
Wangari Maathai
me
you
and every women living her best life had given in to their Doubting Daisies.

How different the world would be! But they didn't. Their sole story is one of triumph and joy. Our Sole Sister heroes combined the power of their foresight and their intuition to keep going despite what other people thought. They trusted themselves and the signs they received from the world and had the faith of knowing that what they stood for was the greatest and highest good. You are no different. The only difference is in your choices. You decide. What shoes will I walk in? And how will I walk?

You see, Dorothy in the *Wizard of Oz* didn't need to travel in a tornado to find her heart's desire. Everything she ever wanted was already at her feet. She only needed the sole perspective to see it.

The Happiest Ending—I Mean, Beginning

If this is the end, where do you begin? The good news is you already are exactly where you should be. In fact, relationships never have a final destination. That's why they always come round full circle—not to drive you in circles—but to give you a new beginning at each end. Each time we make a loop, there is more to discover, more to experience, and more to love. If we missed an opportunity in *round one*, we have the opportunity to experience it in *round two.*

And since there is always more, there's no need for relationships with men, shoes, and yourself to be anything more than they already are—the chance for everything you ever hoped or dreamed of. The shoe is out of the box and the cat is out of the bag. There's more to Soleology than men's shoes. So get out there. Sing. Dance. Meet hot neighbors. Check out their shoes. Talk to yourself. Cleanse your thoughts. Flex your intuition. Eat lots of chocolate. Purge your sole. Envision the solemate of your dreams. Attract whatever it is you want into your life that makes your heart sing. Catch it. Get it. It's yours. Everything you desire is already at your feet.

Index